Good Me, Bad Me, Not Me

HARRY STACK SULLIVAN:
AN INTRODUCTION TO HIS THOUGHT

Kenneth L. Chatelaine, Ph.D.

Edited by

Dr. Norman Levine

KENDALL/HUNT PUBLISHING COMPANY
2460 Kerper Boulevard P.O. Box 539 Dubuque, Iowa 52004-0539

Cover by Dynamic Graphics Inc.

This edition has been printed directly from camera-ready copy.

Copyright © 1992 by Kendall/Hunt Publishing Company

ISBN 0-8403-7720-7

Printed in the United States of America

10 9 8 7 6 5 4 3 2 1

CHAPTER OUTLINE

HARRY STACK SULLIVAN: AN INTRODUCTION TO HIS THOUGHT

INTRODUCTION

The book that I present to the reader has the purpose of salvaging the work of Harry Stack Sullivan from historical under-evaluation. It is my thesis that Sullivan was one of the most significant American psychiatrists of the 20th Century, and that his ideas had an enormous influence on American psychiatry in the middle years of this century and served as the background for the theories of Erik Erikson and Carl Rogers. Since his death, the place of Sullivan in the history of American psychiatry has suffered because more recent developments have focused scientific attention on the areas of behavioralism and chemical therapy. The intent of this book is to redress this neglect, to place the work of Sullivan in its proper and deserved significance and genius.

Along with Erik Fromm and Karen Horney, Sullivan was a Neo-Freudian (though he would reject this term as applied to him). In America, Freudianism has been somewhat extinguished and it is for this reason as well that the contributions of Sullivan has been overlooked. Like Horney and Fromm, Sullivan fused Freud's psychoanalytic insights with social psychology. Strongly persuaded by the sociological thought of the Chicago School of Charles Cooley and George Herbert Mead, Sullivan maintained that the human personality was molded by the environment in which one lived. Sullivan did not abandon Freud in total, but was one of the first American psychiatrists to begin the revision of Freud. Whereas Freud saw the personality as intrapsychic, as basically evolving in terms of inner subjective dynamics, Sullivan saw the personality as a product of interpersonality, as molded by the reciprocal engagement of man with society.

Sullivan's theory of interpersonality defined the self as a predominately social construct. The self-evaluation that individuals had of themselves was a product of social imprinting. Beginning at birth, beginning with mother and family, society mirrored back to each of us a self-image we were compelled to accept. Sullivan's theory of interpersonality, his idea that our self-concept was reflected back to us by our environment, laid the basis for modern American ego-psychology. Sullivan's model of interpersonality was a precursor of Carl Roger's theory of the "phenomenal self." Just as Sullivan looked upon the self as conditioned by society, so Rogers defined the "phenomenal self" as a result of environmental enculturation.

Prior to the work of Erik Erikson, Sullivan proposed an epicentric theory of human personality development. According to Sullivan, every human being passed through seven stages of personality evolution: infancy, childhood, the juvenile period, pre-adolescence, adolescence, late adolescence and adulthood. The European and American mind in the 20th Century was obsessed with the ideas of change and evolution. Responsive to this broader cultural phenomenon, Sullivan took the ideas of process and evolution and applied them to the human personality. He invented modern developmental psychology. He anticipated Erikson's theory of personality development.

Sullivan liberated psychoanalysis from the centrality of the Oedipal complex. Whereas Freud saw the Oedipal struggle as the predominate determinant in personality formation, Sullivan replaced the Oedipal conflict with the concept of anxiety. Although he saw the self as a product of familial-social conditioning, Sullivan, like Freud, also saw the personality as a drama in which early life experiences recurred in the psyche to distort and disrupt adequate adjustments to society. However, Sullivan demonstrated his pioneering reformulation of Freudianism by de-emphasizing Freud's libidinal focus and substituting the broader term of anxiety, by reformulating Freud's theory that basic personality was formed by the end of infancy or the Oedipal period while Sullivan judged the later pre-adolescent (age 8 to 9) as one of the most critical stages of life. Anxiety was the belief that people suffered unrest, threat, instability when their sense of self-esteem was assaulted or diminished. By reconsidering Freud, Sullivan re-directed Freudianism. In the history of the psychoanalytic movement, Sullivan helped remake that history. In the more encompassing history of human psychiatry, Sullivan wrote a chapter.

Sullivan shifted the focus of psychoanalysis from neuropsychology to social psychology. Trained as a neurologist, Freud saw the development of personality as determined by neurological forces. The sex drive, for Freud, was one such basic neurological force. Sullivan moved the center of psychoanalytic thought from physiology to sociology when he affirmed that the interpersonal world was the determinate of personality. When Sullivan made this revision to Freudian thought he made a vital adjustment to the newer 20th Century cultural developments. Born in the 19th Century, Freud remained a representative of the 19th Century but Sullivan made psychoanalytic theory correspond with the more recent advancements of 20th Century sociology. The 20th Century witnessed the change from the neurological to the environmental and Sullivan's historic contribution, was to introduce this scientific reformulation into the field of psychoanalysis.

A product of American society, Sullivan's thought reflected the optimism of the Progressive Era in American history, 1890-1914. Cooley and Mead were themselves products of the Progressive Era. Assuming that the interpersonal world shapes human personality, Sullivan, like Cooley and Mead believed that an improvement in society would improve that human condition. Sullivan was a social progressive arguing that the betterment of man's socio-political environment must lead to a betterment in his relationship with other men and women. Sullivan's Progressivism was demonstrated in his involvement in work for the United Nations in the years just after World War Two. Optimistic, he believed that the insights of psychiatry and psychoanalysis could be used for the amelioration of international tensions and diplomatic disputes.

In the above paragraphs I have lighted several of the more lasting contributions to personality theory that Sullivan made. His writings, clinical work, administrative and editorial career are filled with other original insights, and hopefully the body of this text will make them clear. A re-evaluation of Sullivan is necessary. A re-assessment of his work is long overdue, and I trust this book will help regain for Sullivan the importance he merits. Creative men are subject to the fortunes of time. Sometimes events pull them to the center of attention, while at other times events conspire to make them invisible and rob them of the recognition they earned. This book seeks to return to Sullivan the importance that is his due, to retrieve him from the shadows that more fashionable contemporary psychiatry has wrongly consigned him.

ACKNOWLEDGEMENT

The author would like to thank Prof. Norman Levine for his considerable help in the completion of his manuscript and to Deborah Brown for her technical assistance.

CHAPTER ONE

BIOGRAPHY

The life of Harry Stack Sullivan is a testament to personal transcendence. Beset with family and adolescent traumas, suffering from educational deficiencies because he never completed undergraduate school, a graduate of a third rate medical college, lacking any formal education in psychiatry, handicapped by an irascible personality, Sullivan nevertheless surmounted these difficulties to become one of the seminal American psychiatrists of the 20th Century. In his private life, Sullivan was the victim of numerous personality warps, but in his public life he was a major contributor to the re-orientation of American psychoanalytic thought out of its dependency on European Freudianism to a union between psychiatry and social psychology.

Norwich is a small town in Chenango County of Upper New York State, which is today still a farming region. Chenango County was the epitome of rural Protestant America at the end of the 19th Century, the America that was collapsing before the urban industrial America of the 20th Century. It was the small town America that leading American intellectuals either condemned for its provincialism, such as Theodore Dreiser in his novel The American Tragedy, or fled because of its suffocating conformity, such as Sherwood Anderson or Ernest Hemingway.

Sullivan's mother was Ella Stack and his father was Timothy Sullivan. Both were Irish Catholics and both were first generation Americans whose parents immigrated to the United States at the time of the Irish Famine of 1840-1845. The marriage was not a good one.

Although Ella Stack's father was himself a modest farmer, she bragged constantly that her ancestors were all priests or doctors or other kinds of professionals. Ella Stack was embued with the idea of her family's significance. Timothy Sullivan had no such pretentions in his family's background, and he worked as a laborer. Ella Stack constantly berated her husband for his lack of success, complained continuously that she had married beneath her station.

Timothy was a victim of the Great Depression of 1892. He lost his job at the Maypole Hammer Company as a result and his extended unemployment undoubtedly added to the rancor between husband and wife. In 1895, Michael Stack, Ella's father died leaving his farm vacant. It fell to Timothy's fate to take over the Stack farm in Smyrna. In so doing, Timothy lost status because it appeared that he was indebted to the Stacks, he was the dependent in-law. In addition Timothy inherited Mary White Stack, his mother-in-law, because since he had taken over the farm it was now his duty to provide for her.

During his formative years, from 1892 until 1908, Sullivan led an extremely lonely life. His sense of isolation and estrangement basically were functions of two conditions, one familial and the other religio-national. From the familial point of view Sullivan was the only surviving child of his parents. Two older brothers died in infancy and Sullivan grew up as an only child in a household of an unhappy marriage.

His sense of isolation increased when his father bought the Stack farm in Smyrna, ten miles south of Norwich. Sullivan was three-years-old when he moved to Smyrna and the relocation took an only child out of a small town environment and placed him in a rural farm house cut off from other children his own age. A captive of the New York countryside, the loneliness of his formative years was a traumatic experience which left permanent scars on his character. These years taught him in a painful way the desparate importance of a "chum", of a supportive individual during pre-adolescence.

In his book, Personal Psychopathology, published in 1965 sixteen years after his death, Sullivan left moving descriptions of pre-adolescent loneliness and its devastating psychological impact which were undoubtedly autobiographical in nature.

"The third class of isolation is primarily geographical. The only preadolescent in a sparsely settled rural community is a classical example. This boy may secure some socialization of the ordinary preadolescent type in the hours of the country school. On the whole, however, the inaccessibility of his home___and the ignorance of his family of the significant needs of this era of growth___tend to separate him from gang life, if not from having a chum. This boy always suffers a prolongation of the adolescent epoch___The working out of isophilic tendencies is not satisfactory___Fantasy processes and the personification of subhuman objects are called on. Loyalty is developed to abstract ideals, more or less concretely embodied in fanciful figures, rather than to concrete groups".[1]

The fate of Sullivan's mother, Ella Stack, at the time of the family's move to Smyrna in 1895 is unclear. The evidence indicates that she was absent from the household for a long period, which raises the possibility that she was mentally ill and hospitalized during this period. Sullivan described his mother during these formative years as a *"complaining semi-invalid with chronic resentment at the humble family situation."[2]* He also described his mother as burdening him with her own unfulfilled expectation, as living vicariously through him in a drama tragically expressed in his own words:

I escaped most of the evils of being an only child by chief virtue of the fact that mother never troubled to notice the characteristics of the child she had brought forth. And her son was so different from me that I felt she had no use except as a clothes horse on which to hang a huge pattern of illusions.[3]

During his mother's absence Harry was cared for by his maternal grandmother, Mary White Stack. Harry's personality was formed in an environment in which he was an only child, in which his father did not present him with an adequate male role model and in which he received excessive attention from the female matriarchs of the domicile.

From the point of view of the religio-national elements in Sullivan's background, his Irish-Catholicism worsened his sense of estrangement and alienation. Since he was Irish by nationality and Catholic by religion and grew up in Yankee Protestant America, Sullivan obviously experienced ostracism based on bigotry in his youth. At the beginning of the 20th Century, America was experiencing a renaissance of racism and nativism. The Irish in America at this time were generally looked upon with hostility and suspicion. To an only child growing up in a house with a debilitated mother and raised by a maternal grandmother on an isolated farm where only the animals were his friends the experience of social exclusion based on nationality and religion must have been doubly traumatic. Clara Thompson, a noted psychoanalyst and friend of Sullivan, recalls Sullivan telling her the *"close friends of his childhood were the livestock on the farm."*[4]

The combination of social marginalization, lack of an adequate male role model, the domination of two female parental figures left an irremediable warp in Sullivan's personality. All available evidence indicates that he was homosexual.[5] His first homosexual episode appears to have taken place with Clarence Bellenger, Sullivan's school chum in Smyrna.[6] Sullivan was 8-1/2 years old when the relationship started and Bellenger was 13-1/2, five years the senior of Sullivan. When Sullivan was an adult, he stated in both lectures and essays, that when a close relationship developed between an isolated child and an adolescent of the same sex homosexual exploitation of the younger child invariably takes place.[7] Sullivan affirmed that a close friendship between a boy of eight and a half and a sexually maturing adolescent becomes genitally homosexual by necessity.[8] Sullivan was ambivalent toward his homosexuality but held firm to the importance of a pre-adolescent homophilic (isophilic) stage in human development generally. When he was at Sheppard-Pratt he argued that a homophilic experience (chumship) was a necessary preparation for mature heterosexual intimacy. Only those who successfully negotiated their way through a homophilic state could achieve satisfactory adult intimacy, while those who failed to adequately resolve their early homophilic-homosexual feelings often succumbed to schizophrenia. Interestingly, the two partners of this homosexual encounter, Sullivan and Bellenger, both pursued a career in psychiatry. Sullivan treated schizophrenic patients at Sheppard-Pratt, founded the William Alanson White Foundation of the Washington School of Psychiatry, while the career of Clarence Bellenger took him to psychiatry at Brooklyn State Hospital.

Sullivan's manuscript, Personal Psychopathology, is the most self-revelatory of all his texts. Intended as an outline of his theory of the stages of human development, the book, nevertheless, contains an abundance of Sullivan's self-reflections, is almost an exercise in self-psychoanalysis. This book contains the following clear autobiographical statement on pre-adolescent homosexuality:

"An introduction of the adolescent to sexual behavior is by no means invariably at the hands of his compeers or a member of the other sex. It may be well at this point to

consider the more occasional but still fairly common sophisticated introduction to sexual behavior by a much older member of the same sex___In the case, however, of another boy, one for example who has been seriously warped by the continued or augmented importance of a more or less primitive attachment to his mother, and who therefore is not susceptible to any marked heterosexual drives because of the attachment to the mother___This boy, stimulated genitally, finds in the homosexual situation the satisfaction of the sexual motivation, a singularly pleasing intimacy with another individual, and, by synthesis, a path out of the dilemma in which the growing sexual aspects of his personality and the inhibition of the heterosexual development have placed him.''[9]

But his performance in the Smyrna school system seems not to have been damaged by his excruciating loneliness, or preadolescent homosexuality. He graduated Smyrna High School in 1908 as class valedictorian. He also won a scholarship to Cornell University and in September 1908 began his matriculation at the Ithaca campus with the hope of becoming a physicist. His formative years had ended on a note of academic success.

What began on such a promising note, ended in tragedy. Cornell began a time of troubles in Sullivan's life that lasted from 1909 until 1921 when he was appointed to St. Elizabeth's Hospital in Washington. Events turned sour for Sullivan during his second semester because his grades plummeted. He was suspended near the end of his second semester but the reason for his suspension is shrouded in mystery. Some argued that Sullivan was involved in mail fraud and went to prison for two years. Others felt that Sullivan underwent a schizophrenic episode and was hospitalized for two years and this thesis is based upon a statement Sullivan made to Helen Swick Perry (editorial assistant on the journal Psychiatry in the last years of Sullivan's life) indicating that he had passed through a *"schizophrenic break.''[10]* An additional corroboration for this thesis was formed by Kenneth L. Chatelaine in his unpublished dissertation that Sullivan was hospitalized at Binghamton State Mental Hospital during these years. There is no hard evidence to prove why Sullivan was suspended from Cornell. Only two things can be said with certainty: he never returned to Cornell University and there is no trace of him for a two-year duration from 1909 until 1911. In 1911 he surfaced again this time as a student at the Chicago College of Medicine and Surgery. Even though Sullivan was in medical school, his times of struggle and anonymity were not over. From 1911 to 1921 Sullivan lived a marginal existence just holding on to the outer rim of a medical career. The academic promise of his formative years remained unfulfilled.

The medical school that Sullivan attended was a diploma mill. The Chicago College of Medicine and Surgery was one of several medical schools in Chicago in 1909 with a poor staff, poor facilities but eager to enroll students who were willing to pay. Even though the school was of inferior quality, Sullivan's grades were exceptionally poor. Sullivan completed his medical studies in 1915, but was not awarded a diploma. True to its own character, the Chicago College of Medicine Surgery refused to grant him a diploma, not on the grounds of poor scholarship, but on the grounds that he still owed money for tuition. From 1915 to 1917, Sullivan worked at various jobs, saved his money, paid his debt to the Chicago College of Medicine and Surgery and with his account clear received his medical diploma in 1917.

10

During his times of trouble in Chicago, Sullivan lived on the verge of poverty. Since he could not rely on financial support from his family, he had to work his way through medical school. He did this with a series of menial jobs, and his need to work while attending classes may partially explain his low grades.

Not only did Sullivan suffer from economic impoverishment and serious personality problems, if indeed he did have a schizophrenic break but also from educational impoverishment. Ultimately, Sullivan did graduate from medical school but from an extremely poor one. He did not receive a B.A. or B.S., completed less than a full year at Cornell and was left with great deficiencies of knowledge in terms of a formal liberal arts curriculum though he did read widely. In addition, Sullivan never had any formal training in psychiatry. Sullivan literally learned psychiatry by practicing it and his actual practice of psychiatry began at St. Elizabeth's Hospital in Washington, D.C. in 1922. Sullivan lacked a broad and sophisticated grounding in psychiatric theory, and even after he achieved prominence in the field often committed gross errors of terminology. Sullivan's education was perforated with many voids and it was not uncommon for him when attending professional meetings or seminars to use psychiatric phrases inaccurately or even to refer to diagnostic definitions that were outdated. Sullivan's educational deficiencies were glaringly exposed in his inability to write readable and economic prose. His failure to complete his undergraduate education was probably the most direct cause of this weakness. Sullivan wrote poorly and laboriously and only one book was published during his lifetime. Although he did publish essays during his career and although he left unpublished material behind, most of these works are poorly written and rambling. His inability to write undoubtedly hurt his reputation. Unlike Freud, he left no great corpus of work behind that future scientists could ponder and exhaust for imaginative scientific insights. Sullivan did not exert his influence by his pen, but by his treatment, the lectures he gave and primarily because of his administrative control of the Washington School of Psychiatry and the William Alanson White Institute. He influenced other minds by means of lectures, organizational guidance and personal example, but not by literary heritage.

In all probability, Sullivan's interest in psychiatry dates from his arrival at St. Elizabeth's Hospital in 1922 and his assignment to psychiatric patients. When he first came into contact with schizophrenic patients he was said to be fascinated with them. Since Sullivan had no prior psychiatric training, it is impossible to suggest an earlier involvement in this field. In later years, Sullivan did mention that he underwent seventy-five hours of psychoanalysis in Chicago in the Winter of 1916-1917. But there is no corroborating evidence for this and Sullivan frequently did fabricate facts about his past. Sullivan's earliest interest was in physics but that was pre-empted by his medical studies in Chicago and his conversion to psychiatry was an "accidental"[11] function of his being assigned by the United States government to St. Elizabeth's Hospital. Even after he entered the psychiatric universe, he did not undergo any personal psychoanalysis until 1933. Sullivan's treatment of psychiatric patients began in 1922 and so for eleven years, while he himself was treating schizophrenic patients, he avoided any private psychoanalysis. For eleven years, the doctor who was treating the mentally ill himself avoided the exposure of the dark recesses of his inner self.

The end of Sullivan's time of troubles was interconnected with American entry into World War One. Sullivan went into military service in the midst of the war and his employment by the United States

Government set off a chain of events which eventually led to St. Elizabeth's Hospital and the turning point of his life.

The State of Illinois awarded Sullivan a license to practice medicine in 1918 and in the same year he was appointed first lieutenant in the Army and served on the medical examining board. In 1919 he became a medical officer in the Division of Rehabilitation of the Federal Board of Vocational Education, for with the ending of the war the Division of Rehabilitation started to assist wounded veterans in their readjustment to civilian life. In 1921 this agency became the Veterans Bureau and in the same year Sullivan was assigned to St. Elizabeth's Hospital as a liaison officer between the Veterans Bureau and the hospital itself. As a liaison officer, Sullivan negotiated the relationship between Army veterans and St. Elizabeth's, which was a civilian hospital. This was the turning point in Sullivan's life because it marked Sullivan's entry into psychiatry since many of the patients he treated suffered from psychiatric disorders arising from the war. Sullivan arrived in Washington in 1922 and without any formal training in psychiatry simply began to practice it.

The years from 1922 until 1930 were a time of intellectual fermentation for Sullivan. It was a time of Sullivan's apprenticeship in psychiatry, when he learned the basic craft of his trade and when he acquired the intellectual perspectives that prepared the way for his major innovations in psychiatry. Sullivan worked at St. Elizabeth's Hospital from 1922-1923 under the direction of William Alanson White. In 1923 he left government service and moved on to The Sheppard-Pratt Hospital in Towson, Maryland where he stayed until 1930 working closely with Ross McClure Chapman, Medical Director of the hospital.

The seeds of many of Sullivan's creative advances in psychiatry were laid during this 1922-1930 period of intellectual fermentation. Sullivan was thirty years old when he came to Washington, his career in medicine up until that time was mediocre, he suffered from a lack of any formal psychiatric training and from his failure to complete undergraduate education, but his native abilities asserted themselves when he began to treat psychiatric patients. He had found his milieu. The deficiencies from which he suffered did not dull his creativity. Working in an area of medicine which he intrinsically understood, working in an environment that mirrored his own psychiatric problems, Sullivan's inherent insightfulness and genius allowed him to make several historic breakthroughs in the history of psychopathology. He was one of the pioneers of contemporary psychoanalytic thought preparing the way for major discoveries in object relations and self psychology.

During Sullivan's apprenticeship period at Sheppard-Pratt he began his specialization in the treatment of schizophrenia. His success rate in rehabilitating hospitalized schizophrenics to return to their home was high. Although adequate records were not kept, and although it is difficult to adequately measure the long-term effects of Sullivan's treatment of these patients, a high percentage of his patients were able to leave the hospital and return to normal life. The Director of Shepherd-Pratt, Ross McClure Chapman, showed a great deal of confidence in the work of Sullivan and appointed him Director of Clinical Research in 1925. From 1925 until 1930 Sullivan was also appointed Associate Professor of Psychiatry at the University of Maryland School of Medicine. Sullivan's professional advancement had begun. His climb to national and international recognition and renown had started its upward spiral.

Many of his schizophrenic patients at Sheppard-Pratt were homosexuals. His treatment of these patients reflected his own sense of adolescent outsiderness. Due to the deprivation of his own adolescent period, Sullivan came to look upon the pre-adolescent and adolescent periods of development as crucial stages of personal growth and his theory of schizophrenia was based on the assumption that all schizophrenics suffered from deformed pre-adolescent and adolescent stages. When he was at Sheppard-Pratt his treatment of schizophrenics attempted to recreate the warmth and acceptance of ''chums'' in the pre-adolescent stages for those who presumably passed through these years with an overpowering sense of emotional deficiency and loneliness. He attempted to create for his patients the warmth and acceptance of the pre-adolescent developmental stage he himself never experienced. On the theoretical level, he defined one of the causes of schizophrenia as the failure to successfully negotiate pre-adolescent-adolescent loneliness and sexuality.

The 1922-1930 period of intellectual fermentation was stimulated through Sullivan's contacts with the University of Chicago School of Sociology. During these years, Sullivan familiarized himself with the work of Charles Horton Cooley, and George Herbert Mead. He was extremely interested in the interconnection between psychiatry, sociology, social psychology and cultural anthropology. Sullivan pioneered in interdisciplinary studies and the linkage between psychiatry and the various branches of sociology. He was not parochial, not an isolated specialist but someone who recognized the need to relate the study of the human mind to the study of the human sciences in general. In order to understand the significance of Sullivan's interdisciplinary interest, it is necessary to place him alongside Harold Lasswell and Charles E. Merriam. Just as Lasswell and Merriam explored the interconnection between psychiatry and political science, so Sullivan explored the overlapping between psychiatry and the various branches of human sociology. Sullivan was working towards a general theory of human personality and social behavior, he was looking for the bridge between individual developmental patterns and sociological developmental patterns.

The movement to cross-fertilize psychoanalysis and the broad spectrum of the social sciences was gathering momentum in American social thought in the late 1920's and Sullivan stood at the forefront of this tendency. In 1927 the Social Science Research Council held a now famous meeting in Hanover, N.H. to discuss this issue and William Alanson White gave a speech at this conference called ''On the Relation Between Psychiatry and Social Science''. Agreeing with the thrust to cross-pollinate psychiatry and sociology, a movement that Sigmund Freud himself initiated, Sullivan tried to advance the process. In 1927 he was appointed to the American Psychiatric Association's Committee on Relations with Social Science and from this office sponsored two colloquiums on interdisciplinary study. In collaboration with the University of Chicago School of Sociology, Sullivan's Committee on Relations with Social Science sponsored colloquiums in 1928 and 1929 devoted to a discussion of the interdependency of psychiatry and social science. Sullivan's interest in cross-fertilization remained a distinguishing characteristic of his work and the two institutes he later helped to establish, the Washington School of Psychiatry and the William Alanson White Institute in New York, were devoted to the furtherance of interdisciplinary research.

By the end of the period of intellectual fermentation Sullivan was convinced that society and personality were indissolvably linked. The great accomplishment of this period was the conclusion that subjective personality and objective sociology were a continuum. When Sullivan arrived at this conclusion, he acquired the presupposition for this theory of "intersubjectivity". The necessary basis for a theory of "intersubjectivity" was the belief that individuals interacted with other individuals in society. Indeed, Sullivan first used the word "interpersonal" in a 1927 essay.

Not only were the years 1922-1930 a time of exceptional intellectual growth, but they were also a time when Sullivan made an important (brave for the time) and lasting personal decision. Sullivan never married and had no children of his own, but in 1927 he took a foster son. Sullivan was then 35, and the boy he made a foster child was 15. Sullivan later stated that the boy had been a former patient (which was not true). He carried the name James Inscoe Sullivan. Eventually, James Sullivan became Harry Stack Sullivan's personal secretary, housekeeper, competent cook, devoted companion and lover*. Harry gave James a copy of the only book published during his lifetime, Conception of Modern Psychiatry which carried the following inscription: *"beloved foster son; without the support of whose affection, devotedness, patient forbearance, and good-natured self-sacrifice I would have accomplished little."* In his will, Sullivan left everything to James (the estate stated $250.00 at the time) and referred to him as "my friend and ward in fact" and went on to state: *"Said James Inscoe Sullivan has resided with me since the age of fifteen years, and has been, in all senses a son to me and has my love and affection as such."*[12]

In 1930 Sullivan began the fourth period of his life, the years of maturation. This fourth period lasted for 14 years, and Sullivan was at the height of his power, both as an administrator and as a lecturer.

These years of maturation commenced with his departure from Sheppard-Pratt and his relocation in New York where he started a private practice. Sullivan remained in New York until 1938 when he relocated again, this time moving to Bethesda, Washington, D.C. where he lived until his death.

The administrative accomplishments of Sullivan during these years of maturation were considerable. He left his mark upon American psychiatry not only from the theoretic point of view, but also institutionally. The source of all his subsequent institutional creations was the birth of the William Alanson White Foundation in Washington in 1933. Named after his former director at St. Elizabeth's Hospital, Sullivan looked upon this Foundation as the parent and planning organization for future research and teaching institutions. Based upon his experience in the American Psychiatric Associations Committee on Relations with Social Science, Sullivan saw the need to develop a foundation that would exclusively fund or support psychiatric research. In the late 1920's the Social Science Research Foundation was niggardly in its support for psychiatric research. The William Alanson White Foundation was designed to be the guiding body for the sponsoring of research and teaching in psychiatry. In 1936 the first offshoot of the William Alanson White Foundation saw the light of day as the Washington School of Psychiatry was born. In 1938 the journal Psychiatry appeared with Sullivan himself as editor. In 1946 the parent Foundation gave rise to another research and teaching institute, this one in New York with the name The William Alanson White Institute. With the creation of four major psychiatric organizations in 14 years, all of which shared his philosophy of psychiatry, Sullivan brought into being an institutional core which propagated his ideas. He developed a Sullivanian School through the organization he founded because as learning institutions they helped disseminate his ideas among a new generation of trainees.

Among those who have made this allegation was Peter Campbell, Sullivan's personal secretary from 1926-1931.

The Sullivan School of Psychiatry not only rested upon his institutional creations, but also on his extensive lecturing. The most mature formulation of his ideas occurred during the year 1943 and 1944. In each of those years he gave a series of lectures at the William Alanson White Institute and the Washington School of Psychiatry. He also frequently spoke at Chestnut Lodge, a well-known psychiatric hospital in Rockville, Maryland. All these lectures were recorded and preserved and represent the clearest exposition of his ideas.

Sullivan did give rise to Sullivanianism. These years of maturation witnessed the development of a Sullivanian School of Psychiatry, a movement among the neo-psychoanalytic profession which borrowed many of their ideas from Sullivan. Indeed, in this regard, David Elkind has said that Sullivans' ideas have secretly dominated American psychology and psychiatry. The Sullivanian movement changed the axis of American psychiatry: in place of the Freudian movement with the emphasis on the instinctual and intrapsychic nature of personality development Sullivanism witnessed a shift of emphasis to the interpersonal conditions of personality development.

A major barrier to the dissemination and durability of the Sullivanian system was the lack of a literacy corpus. Conceptions of Modern Psychiatry, published in 1947 two years before his death, was the only book issued during his lifetime. This meant that for almost the entire length of his career in psychiatry, Sullivan did not publish a scholarly monograph. He did, however, publish many articles and essays during his career, but he was not a prolific writer. With the exception of Personal Psychopathology, none of his books were comprehensive studies of a single theme. Personal Psychopathology was composed between 1929 and 1933, but Sullivan himself decided against publication in 1933 because he had somewhat altered his views on many things that were in it. The Psychiatric Interview, The Interpersonal Theory of Psychiatry, Clinical Studies in Psychiatry, Conceptions of Modern Psychiatry, Schizophrenia as a Human Process and The Fusion of Psychiatry and Social Science were all collections of lectures, essays and speeches and not detailed studies of a single theme. In addition, Sullivan wrote poorly. He could not express his ideas clearly and the reader has great difficulty in understanding him. His prose was laborious and his meaning illusive to grasp. The paucity of his work, this resistance to quick and clear comprehension, are two serious handicaps to the circulation of his ideas. Sullivan's prose was the worst enemy of Sullivanianism as a system.

In the fifth period of his life Sullivan acted the role of an ambassador of psychiatry for international peace. This fifth period dates from the ending of World War II until his death in 1949. The Cold War broke out in 1949, but from 1945 until 1949 a four-year period existed in which many believed that the war time alliance between the West and Russia could be continued and act as the basis for future generations of peace. Under the auspices of the United Nations, Sullivan enlisted in the cause of peace and his contribution to this crusade would be the application of psychiatry to the elimination of international tensions which led to war. Sullivan's main thrust was to demonstrate on an international arena how psychiatry could be used to overcome tensions that were the breeding ground for war. It was characteristic of Sullivan to make such a move. His whole theory of interpersonal psychiatry rested on the assumption that individual personality development was indissolvably connected with society. From this perspective it was perfectly logical to assume that the production of a healthier society would result in the creation of healthier individuals. Sullivan became involved with the international peace movement because of this belief. He also assumed that the methods of psychiatry which were oriented toward personal treatment were applicable to the reduction of social conflicts.

Sullivan recognized that Hiroshima introduced a new era in human history: the threat of global destruction had become a possibility. Displaying his humanistic commitment, a doctor who sought to heal, Sullivan was invited to become a member of the UNESCO Tension Project that met in Paris in the Summer of 1948. As a part of this project, Sullivan helped draft a "Common Statement", a conference report, which he published separately in an issue of Psychiatry. The "Common Statement" was a humanitarian expression of how medicine in the broadest sense could be employed in the reduction of social tension and conflict. Later on in 1948, Sullivan was in Czechoslovakia and on this occasion he was again a member of a UNESCO project dealing with the fostering of world mindedness among the young. [13] His final and fateful trip abroad occurred in January, 1949 when he attended the World Federation of Mental Health in Amsterdam. These meetings were disappointing and on Sullivan's way home he stopped in Paris. It was in this city that he died alone in a hotel room on January 14, 1949 of a meningeal hemorrhage. In this regard there is also the speculation of suicide. Indeed the Paris headlines had it as such.

This fifth period of his life, when he played the role of ambassador of psychiatry for international peace, is emblematic of the human compassion and social responsibilities felt by Sullivan. He was a physician and in an age when mutual nuclear destruction had become a historical possibility he felt compelled to devote his energies to the amelioration of political tensions. Sullivan's stance on the issue of international cooperation was exactly opposite to that of Freud. After World War I, in his book Civilization and Its Discontents, Freud was extremely pessimistic, asserting that political conflict was irremediable. On the other hand, Sullivan reacted with faith and optimism in the face of the unparalleled catastrophe of World War II, and involved himself in international efforts to apply psychiatry to the cause of world peace.

But the social progressivism of Sullivan was not limited to the anti-war movement. He was deeply sympathetic to the plight of black America and supported this movement to equality in two ways: as a staunch advocate of black voting rights and as someone who conducted research of the black community and became a spokesman for government programs to improve the social situation of African-Americans. Sullivan's social progressivism grew out of his attempt to unite psychiatry to the cause of social justice: he was the idealist of the couch.

and Rome until the combat between the bourgeoisie and the industrial working class during the development of advanced industrial Europe in the 19th Century.

Whereas economic essentially meant class for Marx, technology meant the means of production. Within Marxist sociology, the means of production referred to the tools, from hammer to factory, by which society produced its sustenance and its survival. Just as class warfare determined the course of history so did the development of technology. The invention of the plow revolutionized the way in which society produced its food. The invention of the steam engine and factory system revolutionized the way in which society carried on its social labor. By changing the manner in which society produced and labored, technology was a major force in the determination of the course of social evolution.

For Marx, the central causes of societal growth rested on the economic and technological realms. Darwin pursued these causes into the domain of the biological, but Marx shifted the sociological center of gravity to the economic and industrial. In addition, both Marx and Darwin proposed a confrontational theory of society. Both of these men lived at a time in which commodities were scarce. The productive capacities of modern factories had not reached the height at which they stand today, and scarcity was a far more widespread phenomena. The primary economic problem in the 19th Century was the distribution of scarce commodities, and in this framework it appeared to both Darwin and Marx that a social struggle existed over the allocation of scarce sustenance. Marx in particular, emphasized the confrontational aspects of a social totality. For Marx, the modern world was characterized by a class confrontation between capitalist and proletariat over the control and allocation of economic and technological resources. The class that gained control over these resources simultaneously ascended to domination over political power.

Largely discredited today Marxism was a product of the early stages of industrial development. As the modern factory system began its take off, as the working population moved from countryside to city, these new factory workers were easily exploited. The Industrial Revolution occurred before the modern state recognized its responsibility to ameliorate social distress, before the oncoming of labor unions which could offer collective protection to the working class and so the expropriation of the proletariat could take place in an unlimited fashion. Marxism reflected this early phase of industrial development.

3) EVOLUTIONARY INEVITABILISM

Evolutionary schemes of social development were abundant in 19th Century social thought. Throughout the intellectual world a faith in the progressive movement of history persisted. Compared to the ancient days of mankind, the progress of western man in the areas of science and industry was both incontestable and something to be explained. Many sociologists asserted an inevitable law of human improvement and outlined, both for the past and in the future, the stages through which this progress had passed and the direction in which it was moving.

The French sociologist August Comte was one of the first to schematize this belief in progressive evolutionism. He argued that mankind had traversed three broad historical epochs: the metaphysical, the religious and it had embarked upon the scientific stage in the 19th Century. This theme of progressive evolutionism was also present in the work of Herbert Spencer, an English disciple of Charles Darwin. Whereas Darwin focused upon the species, Spencer focused upon the individual. According to Spencer, the historical path of mankind moved in the direction of increased individuation. The overall pattern was from group to individual and the overall pattern spiralled upward: individuation took place at a higher level than previous activity based on collectivity.

The idea of progressive evolutionism expressed the general optimism of the 19th Century. In spite of all its imperfections, the advances of industry and science could not be denied. Standing upon the accomplishments of this century, reflecting upon the ascent mankind had undeniably made, it appeared to be irrefutable that the progressive evolution of mankind was inevitable.

4) INSTINCTUAL REDUCTIONISM

Even though Sigmund Freud wrote in the 20th Century, in many ways his work was the fulfillment of the 19th Century. Freud carried on the tradition of anatomical reductionism which was a 19th Century concept. When Freud reduced personality theory to the instinctual, when he saw the sex drive as the dominant causal determinate in the unfolding of personality, he carried the anatomical view of the 19th Century into the 20th Century. He was a figure of transition.

Freud was both a psychologist and a sociologist. We will discuss Freud as a psychologist in the later half of this chapter. At this point we will relate to him as a sociologist.

After he had expressed the major ideas of his psychoanalytic theory, Freud applied this psychoanalytic insight to the fields of sociology and human culture in the 1920's and 1930's. Not satisfied with his exploration of human personality, in the writing of the 1920's and 1930's Freud broadened his intellectual horizons to include history and ideas. Just as Freud invented psychoanalysis, so he also originated the psychoanalytic interpretation of human society and culture.

In five books, <u>Civilization and Its Discontents</u>, <u>Totem and Taboo</u>, <u>Moses and Monotheism</u>, <u>The Future of an Illusion</u> and <u>Leonardo da Vinci</u>, Freud showed how society and culture were reducible to instinctual drives. In <u>Totem and Taboo</u>, for example, he showed how the growth of religion was traceable to the Oedipal complex which itself derived from the primary lust on the part of the male child for the mother. In <u>Civilization and Its Discontents</u>, perhaps the major work of his psychoanalytical interpretation of culture, Freud demonstrated how civilization itself evolved out of the suppression of the need for instant sexual gratification. Culture sui generis, for Freud, was based on the repression of sex. Culture developed out of the need for sublimation, for the need for immediate gratification must be repressed, frustrated and sublimated so that man's attention could turn to the development of substitute instinctual outlets such as art, music and philosophy. Civilization, because it derived from repression, was malaise: in order for man to enjoy the benefits of civilization he must suffer the discontents of non-fulfillment.

Just as Freud's personality theory was somatically based, so his theory of society was physiologically rooted. Beginning from the idea that human behavior could be totally explained in terms of the organisms need to build up and discharge physiological energies, Freud wished to prove that all sociological phenomena could be accounted for in terms of the same physiological cause. Freud looked upon life as an hydraulic pump that constantly churned out energy and believed that this energy was then transformed into the multiple phenomena of culture.

Regardless of the fact that these four categories of 19th Century sociological thought, biological determinism, economic and technological determinism, evolutionary inevitabilism and instinctual reductionism, related to different aspects of the social functioning, they did nevertheless, share certain principles in common. All sought to discover the laws of society. All assumed that these laws are mechanical and deterministic. Explanations were carried out on a causal basis and cause was defined in a linear fashion. If one wished to explain event D, the best explanation in terms of deterministic logic was to show how D flowed out of C, how C flowed out of B and how B flowed out of A. Additionally, 19th Century sociology emphasized the objective over the subjective. Assuming that social laws existed which explained the movement of history and the behavior of man, investigators turned their attention to the objective as primary. The origin of events were sought in objective circumstances, and not in individual action. Human beings were not looked upon as conscious agents who teleologically intervened in the society around them, but as primarily reactive and reflective: they did not initiate events but responded to them.

Reacting against these European precedents, the re-orientation of American sociological thought dated from the early 20th Century. The personality theory of Sullivan was greatly influenced by early 20th Century American sociology, so in order to understand the evolution of the ideas of Sullivan it is first necessary to describe the re-direction of European sociology by a group of American theoretical trailblazers.

In general, the early pioneers of a particularly American sociology abandoned all forms of the reductionism so widespread in Europe. Rather than think in terms of biological, economic or instinctual reductionism, the re-orientation of sociological thought in America focused upon the social. It was neither the anatomical nor the technological that determined the march of society, but rather society or the huge labyrinth of human relationships. Abandoning all forms of somatic determinism, the re-direction of American sociology did not search for social laws as a means to predict the future but rather the social unique and particular. Twentieth Century American sociology was not concerned with scientific forecast, but with understanding a particular society. In addition, whereas European sociology concentrated upon the objective, upon the laws of society, Americans re-orientated the sociological search to discover the subjective elements in social functioning. American sociology looked upon the individual and society as a unity, as an interpenetration that could not be broken. In re-directing sociological thought, American sociology emphasized conscious subjective factors. Rational conscious individuals intervened in society and helped shape the path of its evolution. Since no separation existed between the social and the subjective, the conscious subjective action transmitted itself into the causal chain of society and helped determine its behavior.

Two American sociologists in particular stood in the forefront of this American reconstruction of sociological theory, Charles Horton Cooley (1864-1929) and George Herbert Mead (1863-1931). Both of these men were part of the University of Chicago School of Sociology and the Chicago School exerted enormous influence on Sullivan. A third member of the Chicago School, but one who entered the scene after the initial breakthroughs of Cooley and Mead, was Edward Sapir. Sullivan and Sapir met and became close friends in the 1930's and Sapir also had a significant impact on Sullivan. All these three men will be discussed in this chapter but since Cooley and Mead were initiators at this reconstruction of sociological thought, their theories and contributions will be discussed first. Sullivan took the seminal ideas of Cooley and Mead and applied them to psychiatry. Sullivanian psychiatry was an outgrowth of the theory of social interaction of Cooley and Mead. Sullivan's break with Freudianism, his replacement of the biological and instinctual with the conscious selfhood, were all predated by the earlier advances by Cooley and Mead.

In his book, Human Nature and the Social Order (1902), Cooley rejected the 19th Century sociological idea of a separation between the individual and society. At the core of the American re-orientation of sociological thought was the belief of an indissolvable unity between man and society. Because of this reciprocal relationship between man and society, the cultural patterning of personality took place. In other words, the concept of the self was a social construct. The image that people had of themselves was a reflection of the image that society had of those people. Cooley represented the shift from psychoanalysis to social psychology. Personality was not simply the product of the internal processes of mind, but rather a product of the interaction that went on between the subjective and the object. Cooley proposed a theory of sociological imprinting or encoding: the picture that a person had of himself was not the result of an Oedipal crisis, but was imprinted on his psychology by the mirror of society. The end result was "the looking glass self."

Society and personality formed an interreactive whole. Indeed the University of Chicago School of Sociology was referred to as the school of symbolic interactionism. Cooley suggested that human personality was the result of the interaction between the individual and the group, the interaction between a conscious agent acting on society and the image of that person thrown back to that person by society. Language and symbols were enormously important to this interactive process, because they were the vehicle by which images were reflected. For a person to receive an image of how society viewed him, it was necessary that a language exist so that messages understood by all could be sent back and forth one to the other. From this perspective, the self was not an atomic, unchanging entity. It was not fixed and impregnable. The self was selfless, or it was in process. The self was never final, rather it was in a process of continuous creation: because the images which society threw back to the individual ever changed, so the image a person had of his own person constantly changed. Rather than speak of self, it was necessary to speak of selves. Cooley used the phrase "the looking glass self" to refer to the infinite process of reflection going on between man and society.

The creation of the self found its origin in primary groups. Cooley was also one of the first to define primary group, and he identified these as family, neighborhood and peer play groups. The earliest images of the self were formed in these primary groups.

The process in which a concept of the self was formed was through role playing. In each of these primary groups, an individual performed a certain function on a repetitive basis. The individual was called upon and expected to perform a certain group task: he had to do something in order for the group to maintain itself and this task was his role. By playing the role repeatedly, the individual eventually had that role, that self, imprinted in his consciousness. Cooley helped to discover the invisible world, that world of mental attitudes and psychological assumptions upon which society was built.

Cooley himself was not on the faculty at Chicago, but taught all his life at the University of Michigan. Nevertheless, he is considered a part of the Chicago School because his ideas influenced George Herbert Mead who did teach at Chicago and who became the head of the Philosophy Department there.

For Mead, language and a common world of symbols were indispensable prerequisites for social interaction. Mead emphasized the discursive aspects of society, the messages which raced between the individual and the group. Psychological encoding could only take place in a universe in which individuals and groups exchanged messages they each understood, and this was only possible if the meaning of symbols were agreed upon by everyone. Linguistic communication through agreed upon symbols became the means of communication by which the individual and society interrelated.

Mead introduced the idea of the "generalized other"[14] into sociology. The "generalized other" was the "organized community or social group that gives the individual his or her sense of self unity."[15] It was that collective mirror which stood outside the individual and reflected back pictures of himself that the individual accepted as true. Mead worked within the discursive model of society, and he understood the interaction between society and the individual in linguistic terms, as the exchange of communication. A President of a bank receives a message, for example, that the "generalized other" wants him to play the role of a risk taker and so he adopts himself to these expectations. Human beings are a product of socialization, and their self-genesis evolves out of the social expectations which are placed on them.

Mead also debunked the idea, similar to Cooley, that the self was nuclear and adamantine. A self could be broken up into many selves. An individual could have one personality in his family, another on his job and a third in his hobby. In order to account for the multiplicity of selves, Mead drew a distinction between "I" and "Me". The "I" was the impulsive tendency within, it was the continuity which is a presupposition of any selfhood. The "Me" was the "looking-glass self", it was the generalized image of the person that the person accepted. The "Me" was that part of the self that was not "I", or that was the encoded and imprinted.

Social interactionism looked upon man as a rational active organism that intervened in the society around him. It understood the self-genesis of personality as a process in which the individual took over from the "generalized other" the entirety of social attitudes, the roles and images that the "generalized other" expects of him. Social interactionism emphasized the dialogic relationship between man and society and recognized that because the process of socialization expected the individual to assume and play many roles it was more proper to speak of a multiplicity of selves than of a nuclear self.

Edward Sapir of the Chicago School was another academic who exerted great influence on Sullivan. Sapir was not American by birth, but was born in Germany and came to the United States in 1889. He was invited to the university of Chicago in 1925 where he came into contact with Mead and other members of the Chicago School. Sapir was not a sociologist but a psychological anthropologist instead, but his work focused upon the cultural determination of personality.

According to Sapir, psychological anthropology, as distinct from cultural anthropology, studied the behavior of societies through the behavior of their individual members. He believed that culture existed only in the minds of individuals and therefore could only be understood in terms of the ideas and feelings and actions of the individuals who made up society. Psychological anthropologists concentrated on how children acquire the mental attitudes characteristic of their society, for the acquisition of culture was by no means an entirely passive process. Each child, according to Sapir, actively interprets, evaluates and modifies every pattern of behavior he takes over, so that culture becomes something different for every individual. Whereas the cultural anthropologist studies the individual in terms of the collective, the psychological anthropologist examines the collective in terms of the individual.

The re-orientation of American social thought occurred during the Progressive Era in American history. A period of political and social reform, the Progressive Era represented by Theodore Roosevelt and Woodrow Wilson, introduced many changes in American life in order to overcome the hardships and distress caused by the first great wave of industrialization. The Chicago School of Sociology manifested many of the values and principles which inspired the Progressive Era. The major theories of the Chicago School were democratic, social reformists and held to a progressive view of human evolution. Cooley, Mead and Sapir all stressed social psychology, the idea that personality was a product of his society. If society constructed individual images of the self, then the way to improve individual life was to improve society. The Chicago School was politically reformist because it looked upon personality as something that could be changed. Personality was not fixed by the borders of the anatomical, but it was plastic and could be modified. The plasticity of human personality opened up the possibility that it could be changed for the better. Social psychology in general gave rise to this hope: the modification of society led to the modification of individual behaviors through the modification of his self-image.

The work of Sullivan also reflected this socially progressive attitude of Cooley and Mead. Influenced by the ideas of social interactionism, Sullivan also believed that the reform of society was the necessary antecedent step to modification of human behavior. He was a champion in the cause of Black Americans for equal rights. His activities after World War II were also expressive of his commitment to political progressivism. He involved himself in those activities of the United Nation that were devoted to removing the causes of war and racial hatred. Politically, Sullivan was a product of the Progressive Era and the New Deal and he perpetuated these principles in the short idealist period between the end of World War II and the outbreak of the Cold War. He believed that international tensions could be reduced by the application of the principles of social psychology: the reforming of inferior socio-political situations would lead to the modification of human behavior for the better.

At the same time sociological theory was undergoing a process of re-definition, psychoanalysis witnessed a similar reformulation. Freudianism was the dominant school of psychoanalysis and by the third decade of the 20th Century some of its major premises were under revision both in Europe and in the United States. Some of Freud's most trusted epigone, such as Karl Jung, Wilhelm Reich, Alfred Adler, all broke with the master to found their own schools of psychoanalysis. At the time that Sullivan began his practice of psychiatry at St. Elizabeth's Hospital in 1922, Freudianism was still the unchallenged master of American psychiatry. But American psychiatry had embarked upon its own process of Freudian revisionism and the leaders in this movement of re-definition were Adolf Meyer and Edward Kempf. Both of these men influenced the intellectual development of Sullivan.

The impact of the work of Meyer and Kempf on Sullivan will be discussed in later sections of this chapter, but it is timely to point out here that Sullivan himself was a major force in the reconstruction of the Freudian world view. Building upon the work of Meyer and Kempf, Sullivan broke with the instinctual reductionism of Freud. Applying the insights of social interactionism, Sullivan redirected the course of American psychiatry: he substituted social psychology for the dominance of the somatic.

For Freud, personality was an expression of neurological energy. While Freud was in medical school he specialized in neurological disorders. His breakthrough into psychoanalysis occurred when he attempted to treat neurological disorders with the tool of hypnosis. In the 1890's Freud went to Paris to study the use of hypnosis by the French psychologist Charcot and it was out of this experience that he gained the insight that free association, a psychoanalytic method of treatment, might be effective in neurological problems. Freud took 19th Century physiology and built a personality theory on its principles.

He was greatly influenced by Hermann von Helmholtz, the German physicist who believed that physiological events could be explained in terms of mechanical principles. Freud contended that all psychological work required the use of energy. Three energy-related concepts are useful in understanding his explanation of human behavior: conservation of energy, entropy and a distinction between bound (kinetic) and free (potential) energy.

Freud conceived of human or closed energy systems. That is, there is a constant amount of energy (libido) for any given individual. This idea was derived from the principle of the conservation of energy which states that energy is neither created nor destroyed. One corollary of this law is that if energy is spent performing one function, then it is unavailable for other functions.

Entropy refers to the amount of energy that is not available for doing work. According to Freud, some energy is bound, kinetic, or "cathected" meaning to "occupy". Cathexis involves an attachment to some deserved but unattainable object. The attachment or cathexis does not mean that energy literally leaves the person. Rather, there is a feeling of "longing" for the object, and there are repeated thoughts, images, and fantasies about them or her or some substitute object. A cathexis might be only temporary, for if the desired goal is attained then there is a freeing of energy. As a result of goal attainment, bound energy is transformed into free (potential) energy that is then available for use in other functions. If all our desires are fulfilled then all energy is free. Thus, energy distribution is related to subjective satisfaction or happiness. The concepts of homeostasis, hedonism, and the various forms of energy are closely linked in Freud's theory. If an organism is in equilibrium (homeostasis), then all energy is free, and the maximum pleasure is being experienced (hedonism).

The hedonistic goals that individuals wish to reach are instinctive, in the sense that instincts are considered internal urges. Freud contended that instincts drive the organism toward action and are represented in the mind as wishes or desires. The source of the instincts are bodily metabolism, their aim is immediate discharge and their objects are typically external satisfiers. In his later years, Freud argued that two instincts dominated life, eros and thanatos, the desire for life and death. The life instinct was identified with sexual motivation, and sexual drives were conceived as biologically motivated. Gratification of sexual desires lead to a state of quiescence, while lack of satisfaction, usually because of an opposing force, could result in maladaptive behaviors and neurotic symptoms. Freud used the term libido to stand for the pleasure-seeking instinctive energy that drives human behavior.

Freud's central version of human nature was of an organism that constantly manufactured energy of which sex was the primary force, and this energy turned to objects outside the organism for their satisfaction. He went on to apply this hydraulic view of human nature to personality. The formation of personality was mechanical and intrapsychic: it proceeded simply on the basis of the law of the conservation of energy and totally within the psychological dimension of human life.

The id was the first level of personality to develop within the person. It is most closely related to the biological realm of sexual and aggressive drives. The id is the reservoir of all psychological energy, or libido. The id operates according to the pleasure principle, or the doctrine of hedonism, seeking immediate pleasure through homeostatic processes and tension reduction.

But instant gratification is impossible to achieve on a constant basis. At times it is necessary to delay gratification. To handle the problems of the necessity of delay, the id develops a new structure that can come to terms with the objective world, and Freud labels this structure as the ego. The ego plans for long term goals and is the seat of such mental processes as defense mechanisms, or regression.

The third personality structure is the superego, which is the internalization of societal codes. The superego contains the conscience as well as the ego ideal. It opposes the expression of unacceptable impulses. It develops when the child identifies with parents, especially the same sex-parent because in so doing the child internalizes moral ideals and appropriates sex-role behavior.

Freud offered an essentially 19th Century view of personality. It grew out of a combination of neurology and physics. From 19th Century neurology he took the view that the human organism was propelled by the production of energy within it, and that sex was the primary energy field. From 19th Century physics he borrowed the idea that energy was constant, that it was neither created nor destroyed. Viewing man as a constant field of energy, Freud explained the genesis of the personality as an intraphysic mechanical process. The personality was formed by processes internal to human psychology with little reference to the extra personal, the social life of man. Proceeding from the id, the source of all sexual impulses, a personality was erected intraphysically.

The revision of the somatic theory, was introduced to America with the work of Adolf Meyer and Edward Kempf. These men opened the horizon that Sullivan was later to enlarge, the awareness that human behavior was not solely rooted in neurological causes but that society was also a determinate of personality.

There are two categories of influence a person can exert over another, one intellectual and the second through personal and institutional support. Meyer and Kempf were examples of this first category, for they had a strong impact on Sullivan in the realm of ideas. But William Alanson White and Ross McClure Chapman were examples of this second category, for this exerted a decisive influence on Sullivan's career by means of emotional and institutional support. This discussion of those people who helped shape Sullivan's ideas and life will begin with the intellectual sources, Meyer and Kempf, and then at the end of the Chapter discuss White and Chapman.

Adolf Meyer was the dominant figure in American psychiatry between the years 1920 to 1940. Meyer was the Director of the Phipps Psychiatric Institute at Johns Hopkins Hospital at the same time that Sullivan was at Sheppard-Pratt and the two men met at this time. At the very least their close geographical proximity undoubtedly stimulated Sullivan to read the work of Meyer. R. Crowley in his essay on Sullivan in the book Major Contributions to Modern Psychotherapy, writes:

> *"Adolf Meyer's psychobiological emphasis on the individual as a whole and on the process of mentation the tendency in man to organize experience by use of symbols and meanings, were acknowledge by Sullivan to be cornerstones in his own thinking."[16]*

In his own books, The Interpersonal Theory of Psychiatry (1953) and Conception of Modern Psychiatry (1974) Sullivan himself readily admitted his debt to Meyer.

Breaking with Freudian neurological determinism, Meyer included the social as a determinant factor in the formation of personality. He diminished the central role of heredity and began to stress childhood and other social experiences. He conceived of the social as a co-equal partner in the determination of personality. In 1897, in an essay entitled ''A Short Sketch of the Problems of Psychiatry'', Meyer wrote:

> ''_____ the body and its mechanical and chemical functions and the mental life associated with it make out the biological unit, the person_____ . In this unit the development of the mind goes hand in hand with the anatomical and physiological development, not merely in a parallelism, but as a oneness with several aspects.''[17]

Not only did Meyer question Freud's somatic exclusivism, but he also began the revision of Emil Kraepelin's, a German psychiatrist, theory of ''dementia praecox'', or schizophrenia. According to Kraepelin, ''dementia praecox'' was primarily a neurological disorder. ''Dementia'' indicated an irreversible trend toward progressive deterioration, while ''praecox'' referred to the early onset of this condition during the adolescent years. In 1911 the Swiss psychiatrist Eugen Bleuler, who was critical of Kraepelin, ceased using the term ''dementia praecox'' and substituted the word ''schizophrenia''. In terms of Kraepelin's classifications, there were four types of ''dementia praecox'' (or schizophrenia): simple type, hebephrenic type, catatonic type and paranoic type.

Although Meyer at first espoused the Kraepelian system, he began to have serious doubts about its rigid classifications. Meyer subsequently attempted to explain schizophrenia as the result of cumulative patterns of defective habits. Drawing on William James, he argued that ''habit should become the unit of observation'' and habit training the mode of treatment. Meyer redirected research into the etiology of schizophrenia from the somatic to the socially conditioned. According to Meyer, neither the origin nor the treatment of schizophrenia could be limited to the neurological, but must take in account the social determination of habit. Meyer's revision of Kraepelinism opened the door for Sullivan's later work on schizophrenia at Sheppard-Pratt.[18]

The influence of Edward J. Kempf on Sullivan took three forms: 1) in terms of a theory of interpersonal relationships; 2) in terms of a theory of treatment; 3) as a definition of schizophrenia. Before discussing each of these categories, it is important to note that Kempf was at St. Elizabeth's Hospital before Sullivan arrived there in 1922. Actually, Kempf left St. Elizabeth's in 1921, but even though the two men did not have an opportunity to work together the ideas of Kempf still circulated in the St. Elizabeth environment even after he left and while Sullivan was still on the staff. Although the two men did not personally meet at St. Elizabeth's, they met often in subsequent years at meetings and conferences and these provided opportunities for personal exchanges of ideas. In addition, Sullivan read Kempf's writings thoroughly.

In terms of a theory of interpersonal relationships, Kempf emphasized the importance of the ''generalized other'' as a causative factor in the onset of mental illness. The individual he believed, had a need for the esteem, love and respect of other particular individuals. This need was universal and was not only constituted by nature but was a need that was also satisfied by social interaction.

In terms of a theory of treatment, Kempf was one of the first to use psychoanalysis in cases of schizophrenia. Freud believed that schizophrenia was not receptive to psychoanalytic intervention, but Kempf pioneered in this area and Sullivan was his successor. When Sullivan moved on to Sheppard-Pratt he borrowed from Kempf and Sullivan's clinical ward was devoted to the psychoanalytic, his own amended version, treatment of schizophrenia.

Not only did Kempf treat schizophrenia, but he also had a theory of the etiology of the disease. In his book Psychopathology, Kempf defined schizophrenia in the following words:

> *"The repressed, introverted types of personalities have a common characteristic, namely, through the consistent pressure often unwittingly exerted upon them by their intimate associates (family, teachers, masters, mates) they have become influenced to repress their affective cravings from seeking those aggressive healthful constructive outlets which constitute the behavior of normal people. Their sexual cravings have thereby become forced to seek gratification through means which are perverse to the general welfare of the individual as well as society. Such vicious affective circles destroying the confidence of the individuals associates, lead to a pernicious affective isolation which sooner or later makes the individual notoriously eccentric_____."[19]*

Sullivan's own definition of schizophrenia was remarkedly parallel to this. In his essence, Schizophrenia as a Human Process, Sullivan continued the basic outlines of Kempfs' model.

Just as Meyer and Kempf were critical to Sullivan's intellectual development, so White and Chapman gave indispensable institutional and emotional support in the advancement of Sullivan's career. The relationship between White and Sullivan is more difficult to comprehend than the relationship between Sullivan and Chapman. When Sullivan moved from St. Elizabeth's Hospital to Sheppard-Pratt, which Chapman directed, White, as Sullivan's former supervisor, wrote the following ambivalent letter of recommendation:

> *"I have your letter of the 19th instant, inquiring about Dr. H. S. Sullivan. I could not consider Dr. Sullivan's application for this staff because the administrative positions were all filled with no prospect of a vacancy in the immediate future. Dr. Sullivan functioned here for sometime as a liaison officer between the Veteran's Bureau and the Hospital. During that period our relations were eminently cordial and we got along nicely. As regards my opinion as to his availability for a staff appointment, I should say, as I told him once, that I do not feel that I really know Dr. Sullivan very well. He is a keen, alert, somewhat witty Irishman, who had a facade of facetiousness which it is a bit difficult to penetrate. One or two occurrences have made me think that back of that facade was a considerable discontent that might perhaps express itself in alliance with*

other discontented spirits. However, this is perhaps an unfair presentation of his character. He probably is better equipped than the average State Hospital assistant, has had a considerable experience, is a genial and pleasant individual, and I should have very seriously considered appointing him in some capacity if I had really been in need of assistance.''[20]

White's letter was not an unqualified letter of support for Sullivan's candidacy at Sheppard-Pratt. Regardless, Sullivan always respected White, considered him an important figure in his own life and the two continued to enjoy good working relationships in a variety of endeavors after Sullivan left St. Elizabeth's. Indeed Sullivan even succeeded in memorializing White. It was Sullivan who created the William Alanson White Foundation and the William Alanson White Institute. It was Sullivan who, repeated in his writing, acknowledged White as a seminal influence on his professional growth. Even though the relationship may have been one-sided, Sullivan, at least felt that he had been shaped by White.

Not only did Sullivan feel beholden to White as a supportive figure, but White also prepared the intellectual ground for some of Sullivan's later work. By 1915, White had broken with the major postulates of the somatic style in relation to schizophrenia. In this sense, White was in complete agreement with Adolph Meyer and his psychobiological approach to schizophrenia. By 1915, White, breaking with Kraepelin, espoused the idea that the etiology of schizophrenia lie entirely in the mental sphere. Moreover, White prescribed psychoanalytic treatment for schizophrenia patients. This was exactly the treatment that Sullivan brought to Sheppard-Pratt from St. Elizabeth's.[21]

White was also receptive to the idea of the union of psychiatry with the social sciences. In the 1920's and 1930's, White lent his support to Sullivan's efforts to bring about such interdisciplinary work. As indicated in the previous chapter, Sullivan was appointed to the American Psychiatric Association's Committee on Relations with Social Science, and White approved of all his endeavors in this regard. A community of interest in this area existed between the two men, for at a meeting of the Social Science Research Council in 1927 in Hanover, N.H. White gave a lecture entitled "On the Relation Between Psychiatry and Social Science". An implied intellectual alliance existed between White and Sullivan, for in a number of areas they both moved along the same track and Sullivan consistently acknowledged his indebtedness to White.

The major institutional support for the work of Sullivan was, however, provided by Ross McClure Chapman, director of the Sheppard-Pratt Hospital. Chapman received his M.D. from the University of Michigan in 1902. From 1916 until 1920, Chapman worked under William Alanson White at St. Elizabeth's Hospital. In 1920, he became the medical director at Sheppard-Pratt and it was he who hired Sullivan in 1923.

Later sections of this book will provide ample detail of Sullivan's work at Sheppard-Pratt and of his unique and un-orthodox treatment of schizophrenics there. For that reason we will not enter into a discussion of that topic at this point, except to say that Sullivan could never have carried out his innovative methods of treatment without the support of Chapman. Sullivan was given a free hand, and he literally took charge of the Reception Building (as it was known then, for today it is called the Chapman Building) in which he established his own specific ward for the treatment of schizophrenics.

Rumors circulated about Sullivan's ward in the Reception Building. Because Sullivan believed that a close relationship always existed between schizophrenia and homosexuality, it appears to be true that Sullivan allowed expressions of non-genital physical intimacy between patient and staff on his ward. It is believed that Adolf Meyer, Medical Director of the Phipps Psychiatric Clinic, refused to send any young male schizophrenic patients to Sheppard-Pratt because of what he suspected Sullivan permitted on his ward.

In spite of these rumors, in spite of Sullivan's unorthodoxy, Chapman gave Sullivan complete support. It is believed that Chapman almost lost his job in 1925 for allowing and approving what Sullivan was doing with his male schizophrenic patients. Without Chapman, the work of Sullivan in the field of the treatment of schizophrenia could not have gone forward. If there were any merit to Sullivan's explorations, the tolerance to discover their merits was totally provided by Chapman.

In all probability, Chapman's protection of Sullivan could not go on forever. Sullivan was forced to leave Sheppard-Pratt in 1930. His dismissal was accredited to budgetary reasons. It is highly likely, however, that in 1930 the board of directors at Sheppard-Pratt simply overruled Chapman in the face of a professional scandal, and simply did not renew Sullivan's contract.[22]

CHAPTER THREE

THE SULLIVANIAN SYSTEM

PART ONE: THE BIOLOGICAL
BASIS OF INTERPERSONALITY

Sullivan's theory of interpersonality rested upon a biological core. In his attempt to explain the development of personality, it was first necessary to account for the physiochemical foundations of human life. The biological was the preconditional out of which personality evolved.

Looking at the human animal from a psychological perspective, Sullivan believed that this organism was characterized by two sentient experiences, absolute euphoria and absolute tension. Absolute euphoria was a state of utter well-being.[23] An infant that has just been nursed, is changed and dressed warmly and is held tenderly in his mothers' arms, without her expressing any anxiety, is in a state of euphoria.

Absolute tension is that state which deviates from absolute euphoria. It is that condition in which the organism is not completely at rest, but in which some disquietude exists. Euphoria is a condition of total equilibrium, of absolute homeostasis. Tension, on the other hand, is the experience of deficiency and incompleteness.

Tension, however, is divided into tensions of need and energy transformation. Sullivan described this bifurcation in the following terms:

> *"In the realm of personality and culture, tensions may be considered to have two important aspects: that of tension as a potentiality for action, for the transformation of energy; and that of a felt or wittingly noted state of being. The former is intrinsic, the latter is not. In other words, tension is potentiality for action and tension may have a felt or representational component."*[24]

Tensions of need are those experiences of deficiency which arise from a "felt state of being" or have a "representational component". A tension of need, for example, is an experience of disequilibrium stemming from an infants state of hunger. When the infant is nursed, assuming that the mother does not have any anxiety, then the child attains a state of euphoria. Tensions of need can be gratified, and when they are fulfilled tension or deficiency is replaced by euphoria or absolute equilibrium. Tensions of need are not simply limited to biological requirements such as food, air and warmth, but also include emotional ones as well, such as the need for tenderness or the need for love.

Sullivan's theory of euphoria and tension was not only designed to describe the physiochemical ground of the human organism, but also as a statement of human action. Euphoria and tension were organic experiences which drove the human animal to interact with its environment. Assuming that the individual both co-existed and was co-dependent upon his environment, Sullivan recognized that human satisfaction or dissatisfaction could only be the result of a human's interaction with objects outside himself. For an infant, hunger could only be assuaged by the breast. Conversely, infants would experience tension or deficiency if they were not fed. It was the peculiar quality of the human organism that its needs could only be met by objects outside of it. This relation between the subject and the object was the basis of human motivation. Humans were compelled into the interpersonal world if they wanted to find gratification for their needs. The fact that the human organism was compelled to interact with its environment formed the presupposition of Sullivan's theory of interpersonality. Organic needs compelled the human to interact with his surroundings and this necessary interaction was the biological foundation of psychological interpersonality.

Tension of need, however, did not always end with euphoria. Deficiency need not always end in gratification. Ungratified tensions resulted in anxiety. Later sections of this chapter will analyze Sullivan's theory of anxiety in great detail. The theory of anxiety played a major role in Sullivanian psychiatry and so it requires extended discussion. We introduce it at this point because in its primitive form anxiety was the opposite of need gratification. Infants experienced anxiety when they nursed if their mothers were under stress at the time of feeding. Anxiety comes to the infant from outside itself and since the first external object the child consistently relates to is the mother then the source of anxiety in the infant would normally be the mother. Furthermore, we introduce the idea of anxiety at this point as a way of preparing for the more analytic discussion of anxiety later on. Anxiety was a lifelong experience of the human species, and in its primitive form it is purely basic: the infant absorbs anxiety from the mother. In its later forms, anxiety is far more potent for it could cause personality dysfunction. But anxiety is different in kind also from the tension of hunger. The hunger need is specific: it relates to food. Anxiety, on the other hand, even in the infant is non-specific. It does not relate to finite objects outside the self, but is a free-floating feeling. Anxiety does not refer to definable external objects, but to a generalized feeling: if the mother experiences stress then the child will experience it as well.

Tensions fell under the general category of experience. Tensions were among the first experiences of the neonate. There were, according to Sullivan, three modes in which experience could be organized, three forms of the structuring of experience: the prototaxic, the parataxic and the syntaxic.

The prototaxic mode is the rough basis of memory, and it is the crudest, the simplest, the earliest and possibly the most abundant mode of experience. Everything that the infant senses is indefinite, illuminous and discreet. In this mode, all that the infant knows are momentary states. The distinction of before and after are a later acquisition. In this form of perception, the infant has no awareness of himself as an entity separate from the rest of the world. It is, Sullivan said, as if the infant's experiences were cosmic.

In the parataxic mode, the original, undifferentiated wholeness of experience is broken. But the parts, the diverse units are not related or connected in a logical fashion. The various experiences are felt as concomitant but not recognized as connected in a causal manner. In the parataxic mode, there is no logical movement from one idea to the next. A person perceives ensembles of experiences, condensations of experience, but not causality.

The syntaxic mode is based on consensual validation. According to Sullivan, this is the highest stage of communication because it rests on group legitimation. Syntaxic learning is based on the universal acceptance of language and symbols. Only when the listener understands the words or symbols used by the speaker, can he confirm or deny what the speaker said. Syntaxic refers to the social consensus given to words and symbols so they can be used by the speaker as having a universally accepted meaning. Only when there is a universal consensus, can the child, once acquiring language, begins the process of learning in the larger social world.

Tensions are also "a potential for action". Some tensions need not find their gratification in objects external to the self, but can be "intrinsic" to the organism. When tensions become a "transformation of energy" then they become a dynamism. Dynamisms drive the organism to action or are the grounds of action.

Tensions of need are object related, they find their fulfillment in objects external to the self. Dynamisms are function related, they find their outlet in the performance of a function.

Sullivan defined a dynamism in the following manner:

> *"Similarly the ultimate entity, the smallest useful abstraction, which can be employed in the study of the functional activity of the living organism is the dynamism itself, the relatively enduring pattern of energy transformations which recurrently characterize the organism in its duration as a living organism. The dynamisms of interest to the psychiatrist are the relatively enduring patterns of energy transformations which recurrently characterize the interpersonal relations_____ the functional interplay of persons and personifications, personal signs, personal abstractions and personal attributions_____ which make up the distinctly human sort of being."*[25]

Sullivan's intellectual presuppositions were decidedly 20th Century. He lived in an Einsteinian universe. He lived at a time when the universe was conceived of as a sea of energy. The primal substance of the universe was energy and all the physical objects that inhabited that cosmos were transformations of energy. One substance existed and infinitesimal objects that peopled that universe were variations of that substance.

Sullivan applied this Einsteinian conception of energy to biology and his theory of dynamisms. The human organism was itself an example of dynamism or the transformation of energy. Sullivan took the theory of the transformation of energy, an idea that originated in physics and he built a biology on it. His early interest in physics is visible here.

He viewed the human organism as both the source of physiochemical energy and the means of its transformation. The human body created energy and then transformed it. Having slept and eaten, a human being felt filled with energy and so he jogged. Energy was transformed so that his feet could run. A dynamism referred to a physical function. It referred to the transformation of energy that allowed a physical function to be repeated.

A dynamism is composed of three levels. The first level was the biological. Chemical changes in the infant cause him to feel hunger. These biochemical and biophysical processes include the lowering of blood sugar, contractions of his stomach and upper intestines. The physiological changes are the sources of the dynamism's energy.

The second level of the dynamism is the resort to action. Because of his hunger, the baby feels discomfit and begins to cry. The mother responds to the infant's crying and provides him with the nipple. A transformation of energy has taken place and caused the infant to act, and the action has produced an interpersonal relationship: The hunger felt by the infant compelled it to interact with its environment and so the transformation of energy becomes the source of interpersonal behavior.

The third level of the dynamism is the formation of a recurrent pattern. Through repeated interpersonal acts, the infant learns that specific acts on his part produce specific responses. The infant learns how to interact, or function, in order to produce certain results. The term function relates to the activity of an organism when it intervenes in its environment in order to produce certain results. The entire dynamism moved through three stages, beginning with the transformation of energy through the mastery of function, the attempt to control the external world.

Needs were objects referenced. Dynamisms were function referenced. Both needs and dynamisms were the biological foundations of psychological interpersonality. Dynamisms, recurrent behavior patterns by which the individual interacted with his world, gave the organism direction. Because the hand could reach so the organism was ready to reach into the physical space that surrounded him. Dynamisms provided the basic structure of interpersonality: by giving the organism the ability to intervene in the external world it created the possibilities of interpersonality.

Sullivan's theory of need and dynamisms gave us another view of the origins of human beavhior. Whereas Freud reduced life to instincts, Sullivan substituted needs and dynamisms. Freud's instinct theory focused upon individual gratification. Sullivan's theory was a preparation for the human organisms intervention in the world. While Freud's instinct theory remained intrinsic, Sullivan's theory of needs and dynamisms assume that personality could only develop through the interplay of organism and environment. Freud's theory of personality remained internal, while for Sullivan the self could only arise through the organisms contact with its environment.

PART TWO: THE SELF AND SELF-SYSTEM

Based on these somatic determinants, Sullivan defined the nature of life as the pursuit of integration and security. The individual was a composite of biological and psychological forces. On the biological level the individual sought euphoria and homeostasis, while on the psychological level the self desired integration and security.

Showing the influence of social psychology on his thought, Sullivan defined the purpose of life as the attainment of an accommodation between self and society. In order to achieve this accommodation, the individual must possess a sense of personal security. The major element in personal security was a strong sense of self-esteem. A high level of self-esteem was the major factor in equipping the individual with enough security so he could read an accommodation to society, not feel overwhelmed or dominated by it. Self-esteem was the indispensable element to healthy personality development.

Sullivan possessed an optimistic evaluation of human nature in general. He viewed life itself as a dynamism that sought the maximal expression of human existence. A inherent dynamism existed in life that pushed it to the highest level of functioning. Self-esteem was the most important factor in this advance to maximalize human capacity. One of the primary goals of the personality, as it developed through life, was the gaining of self-esteem as a means to maximalize capacity and a sense of security. Personality was the drama in which the search for self-esteem was acted out.

In his book, The Interpersonal Theory of Psychiatry, Sullivan defined the personality in the following manner: "personality is the relatively enduring pattern of recurrent interpersonal situations which characterize a human life." [26] Personality is a "relatively enduring pattern" of learned behavior, or forms of behavior that have become habitual. The "relatively enduring pattern" of behavior is learned from the very beginning of life, or according to Sullivan's developmental scheme of human growth during infancy. Infancy was the first period of human experience and learning and extended from a few minutes after birth to the appearance of speech, whether that speech had meaning or not. During the first developmental stage of life, the primary experience of the infant was breast feeding and the tenderness or anxiety which flowed from the mother to the child. The formation of personality literally began at the mother's breast. Nursing was the first interpersonal experience because in the experience of nursing the infant was brought into contact with an Other. During infancy, this primary Other was the nurturing mother, and it was from this interpersonal relationship that the infant begins to form a concept of his own self.

Nursing, was synonymous with the kind of nipple or teat introduced to the infant. According to Sullivan, there were four kinds of nursing situations:

(A-1) the good and satisfactory nipple - in -eyes which is the signal the uncomplicated signal for nursing, and

(A-2) the good but unsatisfactory nipple - in - lips which is a signal for rejection until the need of hunger is great enough to make this good but unsatisfactory nipple acceptable.

(B) the wrong nipple - in - lips that is, one that does not give milk any longer which is a signal for rejection and search for another nipple, and

(C) the evil nipple, the nipple of an anxious mother which so far as the infant is concerned is a nipple preceded by the aura of extremely disagreeable tension which is a signal for avoidance, after even the avoidance of investing the nipple with the lips at all. So the signal might be converted into rather adult words by saying it is a signal for not - that- nipple - in - my - lips.[27]

Derived from different kinds of nursing experiences, an awareness of a ''me'' begins to develop in the infant. The ''me'' is not yet self or ''I''. The ''I'' develops in the infant at about 1-1/2 years, and is characterized by an intrinsic and nuclear sense of the self. The ''me'', on the other hand, lacks this kind of concrete specificity. While there is only one ''I'', there were in fact three ''me's''. The ''me'' is the personality in a state that has not become specific, but in which three personifications exist. While the ''I'' is concrete, the ''me'' exists as a composite of three personifications.

Sullivan described the three ''me's'' as ''good-me, bad-me and not-me''. The ''me's'' were ''invariably connected with the sentience of my body''. In infancy, as the child explored his body, he learned to distinguish his own body from the world around him. Through this self-exploration, the infant developed a sense of separateness from his environment. The ''good-me'', ''bad-me'' and ''not-me'' attached themselves to this sense of body, to its separate distinctness. The process of individuation, both in the physical and personality sense, had begun.

''Good'', for Sullivan, means euphoria - producing or euphoric, ''bad'' means anxiety producing, or anxious and ''not'' means panic ridden, or disintegrating. The first thing that the infant is able to delineate out of the vast number of stimuli that literally flood him during his early months is the object that gives him food the nipple. At first the infant cannot distinguish between himself and the nipple. The distinction is only gradually made during the early months of life. After the infant distinguishes himself as separate from the nipple, the nipple begins to take on characteristics - the characteristics of good, producing a sense of well-being, or a sense of bad, that all is not well, or a sense of not, i.e. this is not happening to me, a sense of chaos, disorder, impending disaster and disintegration. In other words, the nipple takes on the sense or the characteristic of euphoria or anxiety.

The good or bad (euphoric or anxious) characteristics of the nipple are determined by the tenderness or anxiousness or hostility that the mother, or anyone taking her place, feels toward the infant. It is the mother's emotional state of well-being or the lack of it that will eventually invest all other external objects (the world) with comfortable or anxiety-producing qualities. Sullivan referred to this process as introjection or incorporation. The source of anxiety is the mother, but the infant will interject this anxiety. If the infant incorporates anxiety from the mother, he will develop a "bad-me" personification. The process of introjection is the procedure by which an external emotion is taken into the self as a part of the self. The concepts of introjection and incorporation were debts that Sullivan owed to the field of social psychology: the objective determined the subjective.

The good and evil nipple of infancy gradually evolves into the good and bad mother, who are, as far as the infant is concerned, two different beings. The child begins to form concepts of the first intimate person in his life, his mother. This takes place from the fourth to the sixth month of life and continues on through the rest of infancy and beyond. In general, the infant is developing the ability to differentiate independent aspects of the infant environment. When this happens the infant has taken the first great step beyond the prototaxic mode of experience and is beginning to perceive and experience things in the parataxic mode. In the same way in which he earlier formed two separate concepts of the nipple, he now slowly develops two concepts of his mother - good and bad.

Thus, the mother's anxiety-free, relaxed tenderness is communicated to the child in the way she physically handles and touches him. Out of what has been called the blur of continuous stimuli which impinge on the infant from such a loving environment, the child gradually perceives a person who he comes to know as separate from himself and essential to his needs. He thus forms a concept of a good mother - a mother who is the source of well being and comfort.

On the other hand, when a mother is full of anxiety, when she is irritable or outrightly rejects the infant, these feelings are emphatically transmitted to the child. This anxiety would interfere with what Sullivan terms "the integration of the interpersonal situation necessary for the satisfaction of a need" and further, if anxiety appears at any time while the mother is caring for the needs of the child it will tend to frustrate what Sullivan calls the resolution of the situation; that is, the tension of the need will not be resolved, and, as such, neither will the interpersonal situation. The situation is then disintegrated by the introjection of anxiety.[28]

The personification of the "good-me" develops when the child introjects a sense of euphoria from the mother or nursing situation A1 and A2. A personification is an awareness or image of a "me" that an infant develops. If the nursing process has left the infant euphoric, its needs totally gratified, then the infant incorporates a positive personification: its gratification is internalized as a positive image of itself, a "good-me".

The personification of the "bad-me" develops when the child incorporates a sense of anxiety from the mother or nursing situation C. In this situation, the infant appropriates a negative personification of itself. The anxiety of the mother is appropriated by the infant, and this anxiety personifies itself as the "bad-me".

The "not-me" develops from an ingestion of panic or extreme anxiety. Forbidding or "uncanny emotions" (i.e. fear, dread, terror, panic and loathing - a generalized feeling of I am about to be destroyed)[29] on the mother's part induces a sense of extreme anxiety in the infant. The "not-me" is the induction of these "uncanny emotions" on the part of the infant and their subsequent personification.

These three "me's" do exist in the infant until the age of approximately 1-1/2 years. At that time a fusion takes place. The "I" is the result of that fusion of the blending of the "good-me" and the "bad-me" and the not me. The concept of "I" is a composite of the "me's" which developed during the period of infancy. A person will begin childhood, the next developmental stage for Sullivan, or life generally with a healthy and strong "I" concept if the "good-me's" predominate over the "bad-me's" or the "not-me's". Conversely, a person will enter childhood or life generally with a weak or warped "I" concept if the "bad-me's" or "not-me's" predominate and thus be prone to mental illness.

The concept of "I" is the ground out of which an image of the self evolves. The self is the sense of continuity which prevails throughout the course of life. It is possible to speak of a self because there is a continuity of experience: the self is that which imparts a sense of unity to the experience of a lifetime. A "good-I" or "good-self" creates a sense of confident or secure continuity.[30] Mental health, for Sullivan, was the ability to keep the "good I" and "good self" predominate. Under adverse circumsntances such as death, divorce, separations, etc., the bad or "not I" could emerge causing severe stress and even mental illness. Some individuals are much more prone than others for the emergence of the bad or "not I" depending on their early life experiences with a mothering one whose own personality had been formed along the lines of the bad or "not I".

The formation of the self out of the "I" acts as a preparation for a subsequent level of personality growth: the self-system. Psychological growth is an educative process in which the infant learns certain recurrent patterns of relating to the external world. It refers to the socialization or acculturation of the infant.

Sullivan referred to the self-system as a dynamism. However, it is important to keep in mind that vast differences separated dynamisms and self-systems. Dynamisms were largely based on energy transformations, but self-systems were not. Dynamisms, for the most part, had a physico-chemical basis, while self-systems did not.

On the other hand, dynamisms and self-systems shared certain characteristics. Both could be protective responses on the part of individuals to threats to their self-esteem. Both referred to modes of functioning, to recurrent patterns of behavior.

There were two kinds of dynamism: ones in which an energy transformation took place and ones which primarily related to behavior functioning. In chapter two of this book we described dynamisms of transformation in which physico-chemical processes induced certain behavioral modes of response. An example of a dynamism of transformation was the crying of an infant when it was hungry. A later chapter of this book, specifically part five of Chapter Three, "Mental Illness and Schizophrenia", will show Sullivan introducing a slightly different definition of dynamism in which energy transformation plays no role. For example, Sullivan refers to a "schizophrenic dynamism" or a "paranoid dynamism". Obviously, there are no energy transformations involved here, for "schizophrenic dynamisms" or "paranoid dynamisms" are totally psychological processes. When Sullivan related to a dynamism in which no energy transformation took place, he was referring to a behavior pattern that arose solely out of psychological sources and that demonstrated recurrent features.

The basic differences between dynamisms and self-systems was the difference between the particular and the general. The term dynamism related to individual, discreet patterns of behavior: the dynamism as selected inattention or the obsessional dynamism. While both dynamism and the self-system referred to tendencies of behavior, dynamisms did not refer to the generality of personality but to specific aspects of a total personality.

The idea of the self-system referred to the personality in general. A self-system was a protective construction designed to filter out anxiety provoking stimuli from the external world. A dynamism could also be protective and the dynamism of selective inattention defended, although in an ultimately self-destructive manner, an individual from attending to specific external stimuli. Even though a dynamism and a self-system could have this function in common, they differed in that a dynamism was a singular aspect of the larger personality while the self-system was synonymous with the total protective covering of the personality. While dynamism and self-systems related to the predispositions of personality, dynamisms were particular parts of the holistic self-system.[31]

The primary purpose of the self-system is the warding off of anxiety. In his book, The Interpersonal Theory of Psychiatry, Sullivan expressed this idea in the following way: *"And so the self-system, far from being anything like a function of or an identity with the mothering one, is an organization of experience for avoiding increasing degrees of anxiety which are connected with the educative process."*[32]

The primary function of the self-system is defensive: it is intended as a protective shield for the self. The self-system defends the self against unpleasant experiences. Since its primary purpose is defensive, its ultimate goal is the securing of necessary satisfaction. The self-system tends to preserve the homeostasis of the self through the elimination of anxiety producing experiences. The self-system has a warning or foresight function: it anticipates anxiety and constructs defenses against it.

Even though the goal of the self-system is the production of homeostasis, it can also function as a hinderance to personal change and growth. A system of recurrent patterns of behavior learned in infancy as a defense mechanism, may no longer be relevant to interpersonal relationships in adult life. Regardless of the reason, if an adult clings to a self-system which derives from his youth but no longer appropriate to his mature years, that adult will be incapable of change. The adult will be responding to the problems of today by use of recurrent behavior patterns that were created and that are appropriate to the past. Such a discontinuity of time factors will lead the individual to misinterpret the present, and then render him incapable of productive growth, of being flexible instead of rigid.

Leaving aside the aspect of the self-system that hinders personal development, Sullivan's theory of the self was generally optimistic. He believed in an inherent tendency in the human organism to function at its maximum. Freud believed in a death instinct, the unwillingness of patients to give up destructive patterns of behavior. Even though self-systems could evolve into a deterrent to further individual growth, their initial purpose was the maximalization of homeostatic experiences. Life tended to maximalize well-being.

In general, Sullivan's concept of the self was open-ended and progressive. Freud thought of the self as a nuclear or fixed identity, constructed for the most part out of the Oedipal and Electral complexes. For Sullivan, the self was composed of two conditions: on the one hand, as we stated previously, it was the ground that provided a sense of continuity in life. On the other hand, the self was never finally fixed but was self-forming itself through life. Socialization was the determination of self. Since socialization continued as long as life continued so the determination of the self went on as long as life went on.

In the article, "The Illusion of Personal Individuality" which appeared in the journal <u>Psychiatry</u> in 1950, Sullivan made the following comment on the self:

> "When that is done, no such thing as the durable, unique individual personality is ever clearly justified. For all I know every human being has as many personalities as he has interpersonal relations; and as a great many of our interpersonal relations are actual operations with imaginary people - that is, in - no - sense - materially - embodied people and as they may have the same or greater validity and importance in life as have our operations with many materially - embodied people like the clerks in the corner store, you can see that even though "the illusion of personal individuality" sounds quite lunatic when first heard, there is at least food for thought in it.[33]

Sullivan meant that socialization was a never ending process in life. We constantly found ourselves in new situations: our relation to an Other underwent constant fluctuation. In spite of the recurrent patterns of self-hood, the ever changing demands of the Other required ever changing selves. There was always a different Other, and in addition to the persistence of self there was always the production of other selves.

Sullivan possessed a philosophical psychology that spoke of the inherent drive to optimalize life, of the continuous capacity of life to adapt itself and grow. Counterposed to these drives of optimalization, however, were dynamisms toward rigidification and stagnation. Included in Sullivan's philosophical psychology was the awareness that mental illness was also a reality of life, and that mental illness was a deterrence to the maximalization of capacity.

One mechanism of human rigidification and stagnation, was the psychological function of regression. As a reaction to severe anxiety, regression was a protective dynamism on the part of the organism. Overcome with panic of a specific situation or stage of life, an individual will regress to an earlier stage of life that corresponded to his self-image and personality strengths. Fearful that they cannot meet the demands of a certain stage of life, individuals seek protection from this fear in earlier stages of development. Regression is a means to escape anxiety. It is an attempt to evade anxiety by finding a psychological level in which anxiety does not exist for it. Such a psychological level is usually an earlier one than the chronological level at which the individual currently exists. Regression produces an imbalance or discontinuity within the personality: the psychological level of development of the individual is incongruent with its chronological level.

Regression gives rise to arrested development. The regression of an individual to an earlier stage of life can become, without the help of psychiatric treatment, more or less permanent. Overwhelmed by anxiety, the retreat back to earlier modes of behavior means that the individual cannot negotiate future levels of personality development. If he is arrested at the pre-adolescent level, he cannot pass through and learn from the adolescent or mature stages of the course of life. Unless freed by psychiatric treatment, his personality exists in an arrested state. This arrested state amounts to a denial of life. Arrestation is equal to the cessation of growth: the fixation of an individual at a certain stage of development prevents him from advancing to higher levels of human functioning. A psychological future does not exist for the arrested personality.

PART THREE: TOWARD A GENERAL THEORY OF ANXIETY

The concept of anxiety played a critical role in Sullivan's theory of personality. It was a central construct in his interpersonal theory of psychiatry. Although it was Rollo May who coined the phrase the "great white plague" in referring to anxiety, Sullivan was aware of and treated this human scourge decades before May's formulation of this epithet. For Sullivan, anxiety was the major disruptive factor in the development of human personality.

In order to clarify the importance of this idea within the Sullivanian system, I will analyze the idea of anxiety under the following four categories: A) Anxiety: The General Theory; B) Anxiety: Specific Aspects; C) Anxiety and Schizophrenia; D) Anxiety and Treatment.

A). Anxiety: The General Theory

On this issue, Sullivan made the following comment:

> I have already discussed needs as integrating tendencies. I now invite attention to the fact that anxiety is a disjunctive or disintegrating tendency in interpersonal relations, which opposes the manifestation of any integrative tendency in the work of creating and maintaining an interpersonal situation; anxiety so modifies the transformation of energy making up the functional activity of the infant that work is now done to escape from, or to avoid, the interpersonal situation which corresponds to the significant need.[34]

43

The basic drive of the human organism is to exist in a state of euphoria. The human organism seeks a homeostatic relationship with its environment, one in which all its needs are gratified.

Euphoria corresponds to the individual sense of security. A person felt secure when they were integrated with their environment. Integration meant that significant others, mothers, fathers, surrogate care-givers, gratified, both physically and emotionally, the needs of the organism.

The primary way through which an individual felt secure was through feelings of self-esteem and self-worth. For Sullivan, the primary goal of existence was the attainment of personal security and integration with the environment, and the primary means of achieving this goal was the acquisition of a good self-image. Possessing a good ego-concept created a sense of security because the individual felt adequate to his environment. Having a sense of competence meant that the individual was secure because he did not believe that he could be overwhelmed by his psychological or physical surroundings.

Anxiety was the negation of the personal sense of security. Anxiety annulled the sense of self-esteem and assaulted feelings of ego-competence. It was the power of cancellation, the force that robbed the individual of healthy narcissism.

Anxiety was the scourge of euphoria. It was the power that eroded self-esteem, diminished self-worth and disrupted the integration of self with its environment.

During infancy, anxiety is introduced to the infant through the discomfit experience by the nurturing Other, of the ''bad-nipple'', a ''bad-mother.'' Sullivan stated his theory in the form of a theorem: *''This again I call a theorem; the tension of anxiety, when present in the mothering one, induces anxiety in the infant through taste or touch.''*[35] This is an important theorem for Sullivan because it asserts that anxiety always comes to the infant from a source outside itself. The source of anxiety is always external to the personality and the individual always ingests this disquietude. The mothering one is always the chief source of anxiety and the nursing situation is critical because it is here that the infant incorporates this primitive discomfiture.

The primary cause of anxiety in the more mature person was the disapproval of significant others. When the interpersonal other mirrored back a negative image of the self, this threatens the ego-concept and releases anxiety, which in turn further assaults the sense of self-esteem.

The experience of anxiety acts as a trigger for the self-system, which acts as a protective shield for the organism. The self-system attempts to avoid any decrease in euphoria. But the self-system is also a cause of rigidity and inflexibility in the organism. Although it attempts to stabilize the organism by filtering out harmful stimuli, the self-system is ultimately destructive of the personality because it prevents its future growth. In order to sift out harmful stimuli, the self-system prevents an integrative exchange between self surrounding others and fixates the person at a certain state of development. Anxiety not only leads to a depletion of narcissism, but also to personality warp because it halts the evolution of the personality to higher stages of maturation.

Anxiety evidences itself in both affective and cognitive domains. On the affective level, anxiety manifests itself in the basic types of emotional suffering: anger, guilt, shame, embarrassment, humiliation, failure. Anxiety varies from mild malaise to incapacitating panic. It can display physical symptomatology such as shortness of breath, heart palpitations and sweating and lead to physical debilitation.

On the cognitive level, anxiety causes actual perceptive distortions. When suffering from anxiety, individuals tend to misconstrue what is happening around them. They "misinterpret" the intentions of others towards themselves. They cannot "see" the reality confronting them.

In adulthood, vulnerability to anxiety is directly proportional to the anxiety experienced in earlier stages of life. If one enjoyed healthy early life experiences, the self-esteem increasing presence of the "good-mother", these people will be more capable of managing stress. The strength of self-esteem prevents a person from being overwhelmed and incapacitated by anxiety.

On the other hand, if one suffered from unhealthy early life experiences, that person is susceptible to debilitating anxiety. A person with insufficient self-esteem, lacking the strength of a solid ego-concept, is vulnerable to the incapacitating aspects of anxiety. Warped early childhood development creates a greater chance of warped adult functioning. The effects of depleted narcissism are self-perpetuating.

Human beings are born with only two inherent fears: the fears of falling and loud noises. But at the primitive levels of life, anxiety is ingested by the infant from the stress or anxiety of the nurturing Other, normally the mother. Sullivan referred to the most primitive forms of anxiety as "uncanny emotions", by which he meant dread, horror, terror or "eerie loathing."

Anxiety is the most frequent cause of schizophrenic breaks. Having experienced anxiety in his early life, the adult is susceptible to anxiety in an advanced stage of life. If they again experience anxiety in their interpersonal world, if they again experience a diminishment of self-esteem, anxiety will overwhelm and debilitate them. They can suffer a schizophrenic break and withdraw from interpersonal contact. Withdrawal is an avoidance mechanism, a protective device to filter out further assaults on the ego. The retreat from interpersonal contacts is a way of warding-off the continued diminishment of ego-esteem.

For Sullivan, life inherently moved toward integration and security. The foundations of security was self-esteem. Anxiety was the great pulverizing force, the negation of all attempts at integration and security. Since it produced a diminishment of self-worth, it also acted to block the integration of self and the others of the interpersonal environment. Anxiety caused a rupture between the self and the interpersonal world.

B) Anxiety: Specific Aspects
1. Origins.

The experience of anxiety begins early in life. In most cases Sullivan thought that it was demonstrable in the first months of life, and especially so when the mother had some kind of an emotional disturbance.

Thus anxiety is called out by emotional disturbances of certain types in the significant person...that is, the person with whom the infant is doing something. A classical instance is disturbance of feeding; but all the performances of the infant are equally vulnerable to being arrested or impeded, in direct chronological and otherwise specific relationship to the emotional disturbance of the significant other person.[36]

The point Sullivan is making is that anxiety comes from a source outside the self. It is transmitted by induction from another person (the child is psychologically "inoculated" with it as if he had received it from a needle). The infant's capacity for manipulating another person is confined at the very beginning to the single act of calling out or somehow eliciting tenderness (by manifesting needs) in the mother. And oftentimes, the very person who should respond (by tenderness) to the anxious infant is relatively incapable of that response because it is her anxiety which is inducing anxiety in the infant in the first place. This is so because anxiety in the words of Sullivan "always interferes with any other tensions with which it coincides."[37] It is a situation that Sullivan describes as "in opposition to the tensions of needs" (the child cannot feed properly if the mother is anxious). It is in opposition to the tension of tenderness in the mother. Sullivan goes further and says that anxiety can interfere with the infant's sucking activity and swallowing. In fact, he says, anxiety opposes the satisfaction of all <u>needs</u>.

Anxiety is the least understood of all the needs (here the need for security) because it is the least clearly interpenetrated by elements of the past and future and thus the least capable of being avoided. This is to say that the more anxious one is the less free he is to effectively select a choice of action that will be appropriate in alleviating the anxiety.

Sullivan concludes by saying that though anxiety is perhaps not an exclusively human phenomenon, its role in interpersonal relations is so profoundly important that its differentiation from all other human needs and tensions is vital.

2) <u>Affective Aspects and Causes</u>

Sullivan infers what anxiety must feel like to the infant, feeling that there is no difference between anxiety and fear so far as the vague mental state of the infant is concerned. Fear and/or anxiety are produced in the infant in two ways: one by the sudden and violent disturbance of his environment (i.e., loud noises); and the other by certain types of emotional disturbance within the mother. The latter (the emotional state of the mother) is the most important and lasting source of anxiety. Certain actions of the infant can be understood only by reference to this concept of anxiety. This kind of anxiety in the infant is primitive anxiety and it can appear much later in life under very special circumstances, perhaps in everyone, but certainly in a schizophrenic break. In a number of people, this primitive anxiety of the infant reappears in dreams at disturbed times of life, perhaps more specifically in the adolescent era. In these circumstances, i.e., in a schizophrenic break or in disturbed dreams there is anything from a hint to perhaps a fairly full-scale revival of this most primitive type of anxiety. The understanding of Sullivan's concept of anxiety was absolutely essential for the understanding of his whole system of psychiatry (mental illness and psychotherapy).

But this concept of anxiety is absolutely fundamental to your understanding what I shall be trying to lay before you. I want to repeat that, because I don't know that I can depend on words really to convey the importance of what I am trying to say: Insofar as you grasp the concept of anxiety as I shall be struggling to lay it before you, I believe you will be able to follow, with reasonable success, the rest of the system of psychiatry. Insofar as I fail to get across to you the meaning of anxiety, insofar as you presume that I mean just what you think anxiety is, I shall have failed to communicate my ideas (1953, p. 8).[38]

3) Uncanny Emotion

The affective aspect of the most primitive type of anxiety Sullivan labels uncanny emotion. Under this title, he lists a large number of feelings and emotions, the most commonly experienced of which is awe. Everyone has had some experience with awe. It simply means that you are unusually and emotionally overpowered by what you see, hear and experience. Examples of this would be standing for the first time in the center of the Cathedral of Chartes, gazing for the first time into the Grand Canyon, or hearing for the first time in full symphony and chorus Handel's Hallelujah chorus. This sense of awe is the most common and the least disturbing of what Sullivan means by uncanny emotions. The rest are less well-known and for the most part quite painful psychologically. He lists them as: dread (much more intense than in the conventional sense), horror, loathing and terror. All these manifestations of uncanny emotions have "a sort of shuddery, not-of-this-earth, component" which he believes is a curious survival from very early emotional experience. When one experiences this kind of anxiety as an adult, it is as if the world were in some way different. In such a circumstance, your skin would probably start to crawl. It would truly be a terribly unpleasant moment. And if we were to experience a great deal more of such emotions, we would be "very far from a going concern" as long as we had it. This is the nearest that he can come in hinting at what he surmises infants undergo when they are severely anxious. The same, in his estimation, would be so for schizophrenics and for people who suffer disturbing dreams or nightmares.

4) Cognitive Signs

Any set of security operations set in motion for dealing with anxiety is in itself a telltale sign of anxiety's existence. Thoughts and actions which we impute and provoke in others, feelings of embarrassment, shame, humiliation, guilt or chagrin are also signs of anxiety. In effect, when we are made anxious by our own low sense of self-esteem it is the other person who should be ashamed of himself, or is insensitive, or is immoral. It is this very type of thinking which is employed as a defense against anxiety (one's low self-esteem) that can make interpersonal living an endeavor (love, friendship, new encounters, etc.) so difficult if not impossible. The ultimate result of such a course of action is to find oneself alone. And in Sullivan's thinking, the ultimate of this, the loneliest of the lonely, is the schizophrenic. He sums this up when he says:

Disparaging and derogatory thought and action that make one feel "better" than the other person concerned, that expand one's self-esteem, as it were, at his cost, are always to be suspected of arising from anxiety...The quicker one comes to low opinion of

> *another, other things being equal, the poorer is one's secret view of one's own worth in the field of disparagement (1953, pp. 379-380).*[39]

When anxiety becomes pronounced, it can have extremely harmful effects physiologically and psychologically. It can cause an individual to distort what he sees. These are what Sullivan would label parataxic distortions. Strong anxiety can also paralyze a person's capacity to deal with others realistically and capably. It can cause an individual to perform markedly below his capacity. In certain instances, it can totally incapacitate a person. When this happens, a person is in the state of panic and if the situation should last for any length of time or occur at frequent intervals, a person can become very sick psychiatrically.

Anxiety in its more pronounced forms distorts a person's view of what is actually happening in his relationships with other people. A person flooded with anxiety cannot "see" correctly and misjudges the actions and the attitudes of the people around him. Hence because of anxiety an individual may feel that people have evil intentions toward him, or are gloating over any distress he has or thinks he has. When anxiety begins to impair seriously an individual's ability to see realistically what is going on around him, to misinterpret seriously people's intentions toward him and his relationships with them, such an individual may be said to be becoming or actually is psychiatrically ill. Some people, in Sullivan's view, in order to avoid the severe pain of anxiety (and indeed, it can be suffering of such intensity that there is nothing quite like it in human experience) will take their life rather than endure it. And if such a person cannot or does not wish to do this, he may develop distorted ways of feeling and thinking that would be termed clinically as neurosis or psychosis. In such an event, the individual is usually unaware of the process by which he is developing a mental illness in order to lessen or avoid the pain of anxiety.

5) Anxiety and Mothering

Anxiety as a phenomenon of adult life can often be explained, in Sullivan's theory, on the anticipated unfavorable appraisal of one's current activity by someone whose opinion is important. When it is apparent that someone is anxious in talking with us, says Sullivan, we might ask, "What would I think were you to speak freely what is in your mind?" And very often the other person might say, "You would think less of me," or "You would be shocked at me," or something of that sort. Thus anxiety in relatively adult people is the anticipated unfavorable judgement of their past or present activity. This idea or formulation, in Sullivan's thinking, leads us into some pertinent and subtle elements of the developmental aspects of anxiety. Take a mother, for instance, with social responsibilities which are engendered in her from the fact that she is a member of a definite society from whose members she may come to expect criticism of her mothering activities. Such members may be her husband, his mother or sister, her mother or sister, the nurse, or anyone who observes her handling of the baby. In many instances, this known or presumed disapproval, this real or fancied fault-finding in regard to her care for her offspring makes her anxious. Unless a person's self-esteem is firmly established and well founded, another person's criticism or even the suspicion of it can be highly conducive to producing anxiety in the other person. Therefore, unless the mother is soundly established in her self-esteem, clear and confident on what she should do as a mother, and reasonably self-assured that she is doing a good job, any criticism of her handling of the baby is apt to make her anxious. Not only this extremely relevant aspect, but such other aspects as her relationship with her husband, her sense of adequacy as a woman, let alone as a mother, the economic situation in the home, all contribute to her general sense of self-esteem. And if the weight or direction of it all is in the direction of less or low self-esteem, then in Sullivan's view, this means the woman involved will be essentially anxious. In such a situation, anxiety in the woman as a mother always presents a difficult state of affairs for the healthy development of the infant. The reason for this is the often stated Sullivanian dictum that anxiety in the mother induces anxiety in the infant. This of course highly complicates the matter for the anxious mother because this induced anxiety in the infant only makes him more difficult and worrisome to care for, resulting in a highly vicious circle that can only have a disastrous outcome as far as the developing or emerging personality of the infant is concerned.

The implications of this vicious circle in the relationship between mother and child, says Sullivan, underlie the psychiatrist's interest in the dynamic composition of the family group in which a patient's infancy was spent. How many components of anxiety were present in the total make-up of the mother's relationship to the infant? In other words, how many factors were present in her personality and immediate environment to cause her to be or not to be an anxious mother?

Sullivan in no sense wishes to place the full responsibility of the inducement of anxiety in the infant on the part of the mother alone. True, by nature, by culture, and by social convention, she plays, in most cases, the chief role in the mothering process. But there are or may be other persons, other factors, other variables involved.

> *Consideration of the composition of the family group may indicate that persons other than the mother may have exerted great influence on the earliest phase of the developmental history, long before these other persons enter into significant, direct, interpersonal relations with the infant. Moreover, in a good many instances, some person other than the mother does have recurring, significant, direct, interpersonal relations with even the young infant (1953, p. 115).[40]*

6) Anxiety and Self-Esteem

By this Sullivan means that a person's self-image or personification of himself is not very high in comparison with his personifications of significant other people. By low self-esteem, Sullivan understands certain unfortunate experiences with others, especially significant others that were a threat to one's security and thus the cause of anxiety. In more adult years this experience is manifest as customarily low self-esteem. If one customarily entertains a low opinion of himself, he will not be able to manifest what Sullivan calls "conjunctive motivations," by which he means the satisfaction of those impulses which integrate situations in which needs can be satisfied and security enhanced. The classic example of "conjunctive motivation" is love which has its roots in the many tendencies that make up the need for intimacy. And intimacy, especially heterosexual intimacy, was one of the greatest safeguards for mental health that he knew of. A person with low self-esteem (caused by anxiety in the first place) would find it difficult to manifest "conjunctive motivations," to find himself comfortably able to manifest good feelings toward another person. In effect he would find it difficult to really love another person and to be loved in return. This, in the long run, would only increase the person's low self-esteem and thus his anxiety. As in most matters of this kind in the Sullivanian scheme of things, the person finds himself trapped in a vicious circle.

People who find themselves caught in this circle of low self-esteem and anxiety try to minimize their anxiety by concealments, social isolation by exploitive attitudes, and substitutive processes. They may even attempt to minimize their anxiety in this regard by dissociative processes.

Sullivan also felt that people who manifested their anxiety by low self-esteem tended to seek out people who would dominate, exploit and even humiliate them.

Anxiety can greatly distort a realistic view of oneself. People, says Sullivan, have come to hold views of themselves which are so far from valid that these views are constantly being contradicted by reality. But nothing is really done in terms of accepting the reality for what it is because of the interference of anxiety. A case in point would be the individual who is adequate, perhaps superior, in his mental ability but cannot accept his academic achievements as real because of the great anxiety connected with success in this regard. This course of events could have been the result of some voiced or indicated attitude on the part of the mother (the original source of his security) that he should not exceed certain bounds of achievement or excellence which might be threatening to her as a woman on the part of any man.

Anxiety will stop almost anybody in his tracks. When it is severe it has almost the effect of a blow on the head, and the frightening and debilitating part of the whole matter is that one isn't really clear on the exact situation in which the anxiety occurred. So painful is anxiety, so much do people want to avoid it, that in the later stages of personality development especially people become what Sullivan calls extremely agile at recognizing and responding to minor hints of anxiety. Just a little bit of anxiety will turn a person away from any situation that might occasion it.

Again, this is why people get such a false view of themselves and others. The distorting potentialities of anxiety are great and the chief factor in difficulties in being with others. Such distortions of self, people and living, can only be corrected through help - through psychiatric or similar experience which will enable most people to withstand certain amounts of anxiety in their interpersonal relations. Though present and operable throughout life, anxiety has a somewhat greater impact during adolescence because of other intervening variables, such as sex and the identity problem.

To be able to withstand some anxiety, is, in Sullivan's view, a way of saying that a person is able to observe previously ignored and misinterpreted experiences in such a fashion that his formulation of himself can become more realistic. The difficulty in this as far as therapy is concerned, is that the person who is suffering from great anxiety and is experiencing serious difficulties in living with people has no overwhelming conviction of the necessity for change. In fact, he expects to go on indefinitely as he is. He feels that he cannot do anything about it. And when it is pointed out to him that he might do something about it, such a person gets even more anxious and so he avoids you. This is why Sullivan felt that the anxious neurotic and the obsessional person (one who has great anxiety but is "hiding" it through his symptoms) were so hard to treat.

Now since people with chronically low self-esteem are involved in these situations, the situations are apt to be somewhat unpleasant and complex for the other people involved - particularly if the other people are prone to find themselves in relationships in which domineering and vassalizing their fellows is their source of security. Under those circumstances, the passive-dependent people fall very readily into the orbit of these others, and all concerned do a great deal for one another without any particular satisfaction (1953, p. 352).[41]

Finally, on this subject of low self-esteem, Sullivan feels that a large number of people who appear to go to rather extraordinary lengths to get themselves imposed on, abused, and humiliated do it for a very good and definite reason. The thing that everybody wants more than anything else is to feel secure, to feel they can handle anxiety. These people who get themselves abused and so on, are indirectly getting other people involved in doing something "useful" for them that will give them a sense of "psychological safety," a sense that they can cope with anxiety, perverted as it may seem.

7) Restrictions on Living

A second specific effect of anxiety is what Sullivan calls restrictions in the freedom of living. By this Sullivan means getting at least partial satisfaction for what one's anxieties prevent. An example of this would be sleep disorders from which some twenty to thirty million people suffer in this country. But such "adjustments" do not allow for what Sullivan calls the discharging of dangerous accumulations of tensions. In other words, some people are just too anxious or threatened to go to sleep, because of whatever terror or threats sleep or dreams hold for them.

Restrictions in freedom of living are also manifest in restricted contact with others (the supreme example of which would be in Sullivan's mind, the schizophrenic way of life), and restriction of interest. Sullivan views this restricted contact with others because of anxiety as particularly detrimental to personality during the developmental years because it denies oneself a great deal of useful educative and consensual validating of experience with others necessary for the growth and development that leads to intimacy. The importance of this process is clear if we realize that intimacy is the core of our interpersonal capacity, and, as such, our chief bulwark against anxiety. Briefly, in Sullivan's scheme, if we are anxious (or have low self-esteem) we cannot be intimate or adequate in our interpersonal relations, which, in turn, makes us feel more isolated and, as such, more anxious, thus paving the way for neurosis, psychosis or mental illness.

In Sullivan's thinking the reason why many people do not get very far in personality development (maturity) is primarily because of anxiety which also includes the self-system (the defense against anxiety) operating within the personality. This self-system controls awareness of what is really going on to such an extent that change is virtually impossible in spite of objective opportunities for observing and analyzing, and learning and changing.

In Sullivan's thinking the less anxious we are made by interpersonal situations, the less the self-system has to operate, the freer we are to become ourselves, free and open to interpersonal action with others which is not only satisfying in itself, but a sign of maturity and development. On the other hand, when anxiety with its felt-aspects is present, when we are threatened in our self-esteem, then the self-system (defensive measures, such as selective inattention, anger, fatigue, etc.) dominates and paralyzes the personality especially in its ability to interact reasonably and fullfillingly with other personalities.

8) American Psychiatry and Anxiety

For years, says Sullivan, the centricity of anxiety in mental sickness has been neglected by psychiatrists and other "healers" of the mentally sick. The lamentable lack of success proves their mistake. In his mind, much psychiatry and clinical psychology has no more insight into the causes of mental illness than did the somaticists and neurologists of the previous century (and for that matter the neurologists and behaviorists of today). The clue, the answer to most of the symptoms that are presented to the psychiatrist, is what he calls the susceptibility, the vulnerability to anxiety, which "calls out" the symptom. Only when one begins to look for anxiety or the vulnerability to anxiety does the real problem surface and then the picture becomes much different and a lot of foolishness in treatment is done away with. As such he cannot stress enough the power of anxiety in causing mental illness including most of the forms which have been labeled differently.

> *In attempting to outline this whole system of psychiatry, I want to stress from the very beginning the paralyzing power of anxiety. I believe that it is fairly safe to say that anybody and everybody devotes much of his lifetime, a great deal of his energy - talking loosely - and a good part of his effort in dealing with others, to avoiding more anxiety than he already has and, if possible, to getting rid of this anxiety. Many things which seem to be independent entities, processes, or what not, are seen to be, from the standpoint of the theory of anxiety, various techniques for minimizing or avoiding anxiety in living (1953, p. 11).[42]*

He justifies these conclusions and the central role of anxiety in mental illness with this statement:

> *But I think that a grasp of the concept of anxiety - and seeing where it fits into the development of a person's living - will save a great deal of psychiatric effort if one is a therapist, and prevent a great many commonplace stupidities if one chooses to use psychiatry in other ways (1953, pp. 11-12).[43]*

C) Anxiety and Schizophrenia

As we have seen, Sullivan believed that the ideas of the several "me's" (good-me, bad-me, not-me) were determined to a great extent by the mother or her surrogate. He also believed that the father played a secondary, but important role in the evolution of an individual "I". If the concept of the "I" is anxiety-ridden, if the "I" is overburdened with excessive negative images of the self, this is the beginning of personality disorders. The infant had developed a personality warp.

In addition, the child may experience sexual problems in his pre-adolescent stage. Because of his over-dependent relationship to his mother, the pre-adolescent or adolescent may have great difficulty in establishing satisfactory heterosexual contacts. These need not be contacts which culminate in sexual intercourse, but contacts that should be emotionally gratifying and that encourage the pre-adolescent or adolescent to continue to seek out heterosexual relationships. Frustrated in his dealings with members of the opposite sex, the pre-adolescent will break off all heterosexual contact. Such a boy will not be able to progress smoothly to biologically ordained heterosexuality. As a result, he may be crippled in all of his future interpersonal relations. This course of events will be especially evident in the mid-adolescent stage of personality growth where heterosexual activity and interaction is the norm. In treating young male schizophrenics, Sullivan maintained that any boy's lack of success in making the heterosexual adjustment was of prime importance in causing the schizophrenic break.

The failure to make an adequate pre-adolescent heterosexual adjustment acts to arrest the growth of the individual at early developmental levels. In other words, rather than advance to adulthood the anxiety of the pre-adolescent years imprison the child in the pre-adolescent or adolescent stage. Anxiety arrests the future growth of the individual and he is a captive of a fairly early stage of personality growth.

Because they cannot make satisfactory heterosexual contact, the anxiety-ridden pre-adolescent finds that his status among his peers is endangered. This pre-adolescent must do something, Sullivan says, to preserve his self-respect. He must either resort to lies about his sexual life or cut himself off from the general gang and continue a non-heterosexual sociability with other such handicapped (non-developed) individuals. The outcome of such circumstances, because of the increasing pressure of the sexual drive, could be a homosexual way of life. Or if it does not take that form, such young people evade the pressures of maturation by regressing to an earlier type of interpersonal living which will be a renewed dependence on the parental and related adult environment. Sullivan said that he found all schizophrenics to conform to this mode of regression.

Schizophrenia, for Sullivan, was the inability to advance beyond a relatively primitive stage of personality development. The individual remained a perpetual captive to pre-adolescence or even earlier more primitive stages of development.

D) <u>Anxiety and Treatment</u>

In his Sheppard-Pratt years, Sullivan originated a form of therapy that came to be called "milieu therapy". However, we shall not discuss "milieu therapy" at this point since it will be discussed at length in Part 6 of this chapter.

It is only necessary to point out in this context that Sullivan's treatment of schizophrenics was designed to relieve anxiety. His ward at Sheppard-Pratt was designed to allow his patients to work through their past experiences and identities (personification of good-me, bad-me, not-me) so as to establish their linkage with present realities. In other words, Sullivan's thinking was that one must come to terms with his "childish" responses to "the family of the past" in order to free him from their domination in the present. Sullivan wished to smash the need for regression and he did this by attempting to make contact with and to alleviate the anxieties of the past. Sullivan's ward at Sheppard-Pratt was patient-centered, and every effort was made to create a warm and encouraging environment. The strategy behind such a milieu was to try to redress the anxiety of pre-adolescence through the acceptance and self-esteem of today, and in so doing to free the personality from the warp in which it was ensnared so it could break loose of the past and commence its progress up the developmental ladder.

Sullivan's explorations into the concept of anxiety significantly enlarged the importance of this idea as an instrument of psychiatric therapy. Although Sullivan was unique in his creative use of the idea of anxiety, he did not originate it. Freud initiated the use of this concept and Sullivan acknowledged his indebtedness to the founder of modern psychoanalysis. However, Freud's definition of anxiety passed through two stages, an earlier and a later formulation, and his definition of the term changed between the earlier and the later formulation.

Freud's first major discussion of anxiety occurred in 1895. At this time he viewed anxiety as blocked or inhibited libido. He was influenced by C. T. Fechner's fundamental principle of constancy according to which there was an inherent tendency in the nervous system to reduce or at least to keep constant the amount of excitation present therein. With this principle of Fechner's in mind, Freud, in his early years, made the clinical discovery that in cases of anxiety neurosis where there was some interference with the discharge of sexual tension it was natural to conclude that the accumulated excitation was finding its way out in the transformed shape of anxiety. He regarded this transformation as a purely physical process without any psychological determinants. Freud maintained this theory for many years and even his final view of anxiety retained some of the elements of his original view.

Freud's later and second theory of anxiety was expounded in his 1926 book Inhibitions, Symptoms and Anxiety. He considered the complex of sensory, motor and physiological experience which flood the immature nervous system of the infant at birth to be a prototype of all later anxiety reactions. The first anxiety reaction was an ungoverned automatic reaction to what can be thought of as the most helpless state in which the human organism will ever find itself. The new born human organism has learned few (if any) ways of dealing with this state of helplessness and so has no way of warding off the intense and probably painful respiratory and cardiac reactions which happen automatically to all members of our species at this particular time. But as the organism matures a most important and mysterious transition takes place. More and more the anxious reaction no longer automatically occurs in regard to a dangerous or painful situation which is actually present. Instead, anxiety somehow comes to occur in modified form before the onset of the painful stimulation. Thus, anxiety takes on a signaling function which warns of the impending danger and enables the individual to employ preventive measures in order to avoid the experience of intense pain. As a result, the ego learns to react to these danger signals in a variety of ways which are probably both constitutionally and environmentally determined. It would also seem that these early learned reactions to anxiety constitute the basic determinants of personality. For the most part these learned reactions to anxiety are what Freud called defensive maneuvers and may be adaptive or maladaptive in different situations. When the defensive processes employed by an individual are varied and flexible chances are that they will be adaptive in most situations. But when an individual's defensive structure is rigid, it follows that his defensive reactions will most likely not be appropriate to a particular situation and will thus interfere with his adaptive social functioning.

Just as Freud understood anxiety as a trigger for defense mechanisms, so Sullivan saw anxiety as activating the self-system. Anxiety was painful, and Freud in his second theory, and Sullivan approximating Freud's second theory, saw anxiety as setting in motion blocking measures that filtered out these painful experiences. For Sullivan, anxiety activated the self-system and the self-system was a protective dynamism by which the individual filtered out threatening experiences impinging upon him from the environment. Defense mechanism for Freud and the self-system for Sullivan were processes of the personality which protected the individual from a threatening environment, and both Freud and Sullivan looked upon anxiety as the trigger that brought these processes into play.

Although Sullivan regarded the self-system as disruptive because it was a barrier to the free interchange between self and the interpersonal world, Freud and Sullivan agreed on viewing anxiety as a trigger. But Sullivan's concept of anxiety was more global than Freud's. Whereas Freud saw anxiety as a mechanism, Sullivan generalized it, seeing it as a fundamental condition of human life.

Sullivan's theory of anxiety must be assessed from the perspective of a philosophy of psychology. Anxiety was a universal dialectic of existence. One pole of this dialectic was the drive for euphoria, for homeostasis. But the second pole of this existential dialectic, the force of contradiction, was anxiety. To be sure, anxiety for Sullivan, was not a metaphysical category, but an actual affective and cognitive state called forth by actual interpersonal experience.[44] Anxiety was not ontology, but empirical fact. Nevertheless, anxiety was a condition that effected all men to varying degrees, and as such it was a global phenomenon.[45] Given its omnipresence, anxiety was a universal force of contradiction. It was that dialectical force that deterred euphoria. Life, for Sullivan, was the dialectic of euphoria and anxiety. Life was inherently contradiction, the ever-present annulment of euphoria through anxiety. Behind Sullivan's psychology there lies a philosophy of life.

PART FOUR: THE DEVELOPMENTAL STAGES OF LIFE

This part of the study of the Sullivanian system will be devoted to a discussion of his theory concerning the stages of psychological development. We will begin with a brief synopsis of the Sullivanian developmental theory, and in the later portions we will give a detailed description of each of these psychological phases of growth.

Sullivan's development scheme was composed of the following seven periods:

1) Infancy, which extended from a few minutes after birth to the appearance of speech, whether that speech had meaning or not.

2) Childhood, which extended from the appearance of the ability to utter articulate sounds to the appearance of the need for playmates - that is, companions of approximately one's own age and status.

3) The juvenile period which extended through most of the grammar-school years to what Sullivan calls "the need for an intimate relation with another person of comparable status."[46]

4) The pre-adolescent stage (probably the most important stage for Sullivan) which physically ends with the eruption of puberty and genital sexuality and psychologically ends with the movement of strong interest from a person of one's own sex to a person of the opposite sex, or from homophilic to heterosexual love.

5) The beginning of adolescence which for Sullivan, continues until "one has patterned some type of performance which satisfied one's lust or one's genital drives."[47]

6) Such "patterning" ushers in late adolescence which lasts as a stage of development until those partially developed aspects of personality are fully developed or as Sullivan says "fall into the proper relationship to their time partition."[48]

7) Thus the final stage of adulthood is reached when one is able to establish relationships of love for some other person in which the other person is as significant or nearly as significant as one's self. According to Sullivan this is what love and true intimacy really mean. Although, as he says, it is not the principal business of live, it is perhaps the principal source of satisfaction in life.

Sullivan's theory of personality development was an epigenetic, one which identifies different stages that must be successfully negotiated if the person was to blossom into a healthy individual. An epigenetic theory is patterned on an organic model. A life is a total process which is composed of various stages. The process is an interdependent one, in which the whole and parts reciprocally effect each other. In order for the whole process to conclude with the production of a healthy adult, the seven stages of development must be successfully negotiated. In order to end with the mature individual, a self must pass through each of the stages satisfactorily. Failure to negotiate any of these periods satisfactorily will damage the entire process, for a warp in one stage will mean that the self is too damaged to complete the subsequent stage successfully. A flawed part flaws all the succeeding stages and ultimately the whole.

Sullivan's theory corresponds to the embryological thesis regarding growth. In embryological theory, the mutually interdependent parts cannot function properly in the total organized biological system if any one of the parts is defective. In order to understand Sullivan's theory of the necessary stages of personality development, it is important to think not only in terms of whole and parts but also of ends and means. The human organism seeks to attain the end of adequate function but it can only accomplish this end if all the means, the intermediary stages of growth, have all been successfully concluded.

A resemblance exists between Sullivan's epigenetic concept and the developmental theory of Erik Erikson. Sullivan wrote before Erikson and even though Erikson also looked upon life as a sequence of interdependent stages, it is difficult to establish any direct influence of Sullivan on Erikson. Whereas Sullivan ended his schema with adulthood, Erikson expanded his own model to include old age. Sullivan was primarily concerned with the span of human life running from infancy to adulthood, but Erikson enlarged this vision and related to the entire life process beginning in infancy and ceasing with death.

Leaving aside the question of any direct influence of Sullivan on Erikson, an influence which Erikson himself denies, it is perhaps best to understand these two men as responding in the same way to certain cultural ideas which were abroad in the 20th Century. Sullivan was the precursor, he was the explorer who first saw the relevancy of the idea of development for psychiatry. His originality in this regard must be recognized. But a major idea of the 20th Century was change process and historicity. Recognizing that Sullivan was antecedent to Erikson, both men succeeded in applying the uniquely 20th Century idea of historicity to psychology. Abandoning the Freudian idea that a nuclear personality is formed by the adolescent period and remains fixed and permanent through a life, both Sullivan and Erikson applied the idea of process to personality. They were historians of the mind, inspired by the 20th Century concept of change to suggest too that the personality was an evolutionary process which incorporated sequential steps in itself.

Both Sullivan and Erikson also looked upon the evolutionary process of life as open ended. Growth and change did not stop at any particular period in existence, but lasted as long as life itself.

1. Infancy

If the period of infancy is successfully negotiated, the infant should emerge from it with a healthy concept of self. Ideally, the neonate should conclude his infancy with strong self-esteem and a positive image of the ''I''.

The initiation of a positive ''I'' concept begins in the nursing situation. If the infant is nursed with tenderness and love by the mother then the infant has received the ''good nipple''. The tenderness he feels, the milk he receives from the mother coalesce and present to him a personification of the mother as the ''good-mother''. Personification is a process by which feelings and emotions configurate themselves into a person. Because the mother is loving and kind, because she supplies adequate milk, these secure feelings the infant feels personify themselves into the image of the ''good-mother''.

The centrality of the nursing situation is further evidenced if the mother is anxious or under stress. In this situation, the anxiety of the mother transmits itself to the infant, and the mother is personified as the ''bad-mother''. If the mother is clumsy in handling the child, if the breasts do not produce sufficient milk, all this dissatisfaction is transmitted to the infant and he personifies the mothering-one as the ''bad-mother''.

The nursing situation is also the initial interpersonal relationship. The infant interacts with the Other, and out of this relationship his first concepts of his own self begin to develop.

According to Sullivan, the need for security is primary in life. If the infant interacts with the ''good-mother'' he or she feels secure and begins to develop feelings of self-esteem. If the infant interacts with the ''bad-mother'', he or she feels anxiety and a negative self-image begins to evolve. Anxiety is a feeling which interferes with the sense of security. Anxiety is a block that filters out feelings of security, and in so doing inhibits the growth of self-worth. The personification of the ''good-mother'' or ''bad-mother'' are outgrowths of an interpersonal relationship that initially originates in the nursing situation.

The personification of the mother eventually leads to the self-personification of the infant. The ''good-mother'' will eventually be incorporated in the infant as the ''good-me''. Conversely, the ''bad-mother'' will eventually be incorporated in the infant as the ''bad-me'' or the ''not me''. The process moves in the following stages: personification of the mother through the nursing interaction, the infants ingestion of the mother personification and the development of the personification of the self which is a mirror image of the personification of the mother.

When the infant is approximately 1-1/2-years-old, the various images of the ''me'' conflate. The ''good-me'', ''bad-me'' and ''not-me'' condense into an ''I''. Hopefully there is enough ''good-me'' in the ''I'' so that the neonate has come to the end of his infancy with a ''good'' concept of self. A ''good-I'' means abundant feelings of self-worth and self-esteem and a feeling of security that prevails through the individual.

The mode of experience through the infancy stage is prototaxic and parataxic.

2) Childhood

The greatest advance at the childhood stage is the acquisition of language. In his mastery of language, the child also acquires the ability for syntaxic thought and consensual thinking and learning.

Syntaxic thinking and the ability to use language also gives rise to the ability for consensual thinking and learning. By this phrase, Sullivan means thinking or learning that is consensually validated or socially legitimated. Language opens up a huge new world for the child. It becomes an infinite world with infinite interpersonal contacts. Through his interaction with society generally, the learning process of the child receives consensual approval. The use of language requires that a social consensus exists on the meaning of at least words: communication would be impossible if members of society did not agree on the meaning of words. Based upon language, the knowledge the child receives is socially validated knowledge: it is knowledge upon which there is a general social legitimization.

Consensual thinking and learning is a major step in the socialization process of the child. It is a movement from the purely subjective existence of infancy to the interrelationship of child and objective society. Syntaxic thinking and the use of language are crucial layers in the acculturation process of the young, for the use of language means that their interaction with the other is automatically interpersonal as language is inherently a social medium of communication.

Childhood is also a period in which the young person will act badly. Infants can act badly, but this unpleasant behavior is normally a consequence of the tension of anxiety. In childhood, a young person can voluntarily act badly. Sullivan called this voluntary origin of bad behavior the "malevolent transformation."

The "malevolent transformation" also develops out of the personification process. Only in this case the child incorporates the personification of the father. Based upon his own familial experience, Sullivan proposed that the mother will draw attention to the father's insufficiencies. She will degrade him in front of the child. The personification of the father is now presented as the "poor-father". The male child identifies with the father, with the "poor-father". He appropriates the deficient father image and he personifies himself as unworthy and deficient as well. Because of his lack of self-esteem and self-security, i.e. a sense that he is really not loved, the child engages in a "malevolent transformation". He acts out what he feels: since he feels low self-esteem he acts in a manner that corresponds to this deficient self-image. He is worthy no more. All things considered, malevolent transformation was, for Sullivan, the greatest disaster that can befall any individual during childhood.

3) Juvenile

The juvenile stage lasts from the age of 5 or 6 until 8 or 9. The juvenile stage is concomitant with the young persons entry into a school situation or kindergarten. This is an enormous advance in the process of socialization because it signals the movement from family to society. No longer is the family the sole source of influence on the juvenile, but now a competitor has entered the field: the school and its teachers.

The entrance into school provides a countervailing force to the family: the "I" of the juvenile is re-enforced by sources outside of the family. Mothers and fathers no longer are the single origins of the self-image of the juvenile. They have been "de-devinized". In fact, a good school situation can often overcome the damages of an earlier poor home environment. A positive teacher can reverse the deterioration of the self-concept caused by a chaotic family situation and through encouragement and stimulation substitute a more secure self-image. The totalitarian hold of the family is broken. The converse is also true - a "bad" teacher situation can threaten the good-parent, good-me experience of earlier years and cause the child to doubt the "good I" already formed.

In the school environment, the juvenile learns both cooperation and competition. While cooperation is both personally and socially advantageous, competition can be harmful. Some people are hurt by a competitive environment and a competitive society can cause great individual pain.

Juveniles also learn the mechanism of "selective inattention". By the term "selective inattention", Sullivan referred to a defensive mechanism on the part of the organism, or a distinct part of the self-system. Juveniles learn to be selectively inattentive, or not to hear or see remarks or scenes that are painful to them. If a parent berates a juvenile, the juvenile can adopt the dynamism of the self-system and choose not to hear what the hostile parent has said. They can tune it out while hearing what they are most comfortable hearing.

4) Pre-Adolescence

For Sullivan, mental health was the ability to maintain adequate and healthy interpersonal relations.[49] Within the framework of intersubjective relations, the capacity to be intimate in the heterosexual sense provided the surest guarantee of a healthy personality.

Sullivan defined love as the ability to have as much concern for another as one has for themselves. Love was that state in which a person lost his or her selfishness: the well-being and feeling of another person were equally as important to them as their own security. A mature personality was someone who could love. Sullivan defined love as the extremist form of intimacy.

If the capacity for intimacy was the highest purpose of the maturation process, then the pre-adolescent stage of development was a pivotal stage to be negotiated successfully. This was true because the pre-adolescent stage was the time frame in human life when feelings of lust and intimacy began to assert themselves. Because sexual desires began to unfold, the individual was driven to engage in intimate relations with other individuals of comparable age and status. The primary function of the pre-adolescent period was to establish the foundation for the capacity for love, intimacy and sexual gratification.

The pre-adolescent stage spanned the years from 8 to 9 and ended with the full eruption of puberty and genital sexuality. Sullivan looked upon pre-adolescence as one of the most crucial stages in the process of personality growth because it constructed the patterns of heterosexual or homosexual relationships that were to last for a lifetime.

Pre-adolescence, as we have seen in Chapter One, carried a particularly personal meaning for Sullivan. In these years of his own life, Sullivan probably engaged in a homosexual relationship with Clarence Bellenger. Because his own homosexual preference was established at this time, Sullivan naturally regarded this period as central for future personality development. His own experience predisposed him to accentuate the significance of pre-adolescence.

Pre-adolescence were also years of exceptionally painful loneliness for Sullivan. In all probability, his sense of personal isolation, his poor relationship to his mother prepared him for a homosexual encounter. Full-blown loneliness for Sullivan, was so terrible that it practically baffles clear recall. The utter isolation that complete loneliness entails is almost beyond belief or imagination. This is the reason why there is the driving impulsion in the pre-adolescent era for integrative interpersonal situations (to find chums) despite very serious anxiety. Under the impact of loneliness, people will seek companionships even though they are intensity anxious in this regard.

Sullivan's appreciation of loneliness also had autobiographical roots. As an only child on an isolated farm, he was cut off from healthy peer group relationships. Based on his own experience, Sullivan listed five conditions which produced a chronically lonely person: 1) the failure to experience love during infancy, childhood and juvenile periods; 2) the failure to have adult participation in childhood activities; 3) the failure to have a peer group; 4) the failure to find acceptance; 5) the failure to establish an intimate exchange with a fellow human being who we may describe or identify as a chum.

Indeed, the mature Sullivan who became a psychiatrist argued that in pre-adolescence boys felt at greater ease with other boys than with members of the opposite sex. Pre-adolescence was a time of gender identity, when members of the same sex felt enormous empathy and closeness for each other. According to Sullivan, the appearance of the capacity for love in pre-adolescence was frequently manifested in a homophlyic sometimes homosexual form. Because of gender identification, the first expression of intimacy frequently assumed the homophilic form.

This homophilic tendency in pre-adolescence created a unique type of inter-gender relationship. Chumship meant a new type of interest in a particular other person of the same sex who became a intimately close friend or chum. It meant that the satisfactions and the security which are experienced by someone else, some particular other person, begin to be significant to the ''I'' as the ''I's'' own satisfaction and security.

But the overriding question for this stage of development is this: are pre-adolescent chum - relationships necessary for interpersonal heterosexual intimacy during adolescence and thereafter. Are homophylic relationships a necessary precondition for the establishment of true love relationships between men and women? Sullivan thought so. He believed that an adult cannot love unless and until he experienced pre-adolescent love.

How then, in a very concrete way, would one characterize interpersonal intimacy or love in a chum-relationship in the Sullivanian sense? First, it involves free uninhibited communication of one's thoughts, fantasies, plans and motives. In Conceptions of Modern Psychiatry Sullivan wrote that expressing oneself freely in pre-adolescence acted as the necessary foundation for the increase in the consensual validation of symbols and of information, of the data about living and of the world in general which makes possible a movement away from egocentrical to a more social, altruistic outlook on life.[50]

Secondly, in a chum relationship each one of the dyad affirms and enhances the personal worth and integrity of the other. This is what Sullivan calls a ''validation'' of the value of the various aspects of the personality of each. This validation is brought about by what Sullivan calls collaboration, which is the feeling of sensitivity for another person.

In addition to the importance of chum relationships in pre-adolescence, Sullivan also used chum relationships as part of his therapy for schizophrenics at Sheppard-Pratt. In his treatment of schizophrenia, Sullivan attempted to re-create the chum relationships of pre-adolescence, obviously feeling that the mentally ill patients had not successfully negotiated the pre-adolescent stage. By reconstructing the pre-adolescent years for his patients, Sullivan hoped to give them another opportunity to complete this period of development and to overcome this barrier to their mental health. We shall discuss this in greater depth in the part dealing with Sullivanian treatment.

5) Early Adolescence

The early adolescent stage should be a period of transition from homophylic to heterosexual relationships. During these years, a shift in gender preference should occur: the primary object of intimacy should transfer from homophilic (isophilic) to heterophilic objects. The healthy negotiation of the early adolescent stage entailed the abandonment of homophilism and the adoption of heterosexuality.

The dominant social attitude during Sullivan's life-time regarded heterophilic activity as the normal and moral form of sexuality, and unless one were heterosexual it was extremely difficult to develop a healthy personality structure though homosexuality orientated himself, Sullivan felt this to be true and went so far as to say that the greatest safeguard to mental health he knew of was heterosexual intimacy. Also given the prevailing social pressures, only those persons who choose a heterophilic mode of life could be guaranteed social acceptance, a necessary requirement for a healthy personality.

The early adolescent stage witnessed the full eruption of puberty and genital sexuality. Given the pressures of genital sexuality, the function of the early adolescent stage in the total life process is to manage the transference from pre-adolescent homophilism to heterophilic activity. This shift helped establish the goals of late adolescence which called for the construction of recurrent patterns of interpersonal relationships. While the function of early adolescence was to establish sexual preference, the function of late adolescence was to formulate recurrent patterns in which this sexual preference was expressed.

In discussing the sexuality of the early adolescent stage, Sullivan drew a distinction between intimacy and lust. Intimacy and love were involved with closeness and tenderness. Intimacy was not the same as lust, for it could exist without and independent of lust. Intimacy could express itself in lust, but it had its genesis in sources other than lust. It was most closely connected with warmth, compassion and empathy. Sullivan classified the need for intimacy in terms of the following categories:

1) Autophilic, in which the capacity for love is concentrated upon the self;

2) The isophilic, in which intimacy is only directed at members of his own sex

3) The heterophilic, in which love is expressed between members of the opposite sex, or the socially approved mode.

Lust was limited to genital gratification. In order for lust to be satisfied, it was not necessary for any feelings of intimacy to be involved. Lust related to pure neurological relief. During early adolescence, lust predominated over intimacy. During adulthood, lust and intimacy hopefully combined. Mature love rested upon a synthesis of lust and intimacy. Except for loneliness, Sullivan thought that lust was the most powerful dynamism in interpersonal relations. It was also the last of the major dynamisms that motivated and directed human emotional processes and personality development.[51]

The following example may be used to illustrate what Sullivan referred to as the lust dynamism. As he sits beside an attractive girl in a university classroom, a young college student begins to feel sexually aroused, he experiences tensions within him that are produced by internal hormonal biochemical processes. These processes are brought to his attention through tensions or partial erection of the penis. This physical tension experienced by this particular student is what Sullivan called the source of the dynamism. Over a period of time, he is able to form a friendship with the girl and has many dates with her and eventually they engage in genital intercourse. This, according to Sullivan, is the course of the energy of the dynamism; it finds it final expression in a close interpersonal relationship between the two of them. The way in which the energy flows in this dynamism is influenced by many social and cultural factors. If one member of this couple is a devoted member of a certain religion that prohibits premarital sexual intercourse, the energy flow will be different. If social factors intervene, such as parental objections, the dynamism may proceed in another manner.

In either case, these instances of the young man's flow of energy proceeds in a way that is characteristic of him and reflects his development and past experience. If this pattern endures over a significant period of time, it constitutes what Sullivan calls a dynamism and forms an essential feature of his emotional and interpersonal functioning.[52]

Sullivan felt that the lust dynamism was one of the most important of the human integrative tendencies. The lust dynamism was related to an external object. In order to gratify the lust dynamism it was necessary to seek gratification in an object outside of ourselves: for example, an attractive member of the opposite sex. Because the source of gratification was external to the self, the lust dynamism served to integrate the self with the Other, it served as a powerful basis for interpersonal integration. But the lust dynamism was also the ground for a tragic contradiction between man and society. The social world took an essentially repressive approach to the lust dynamism and so a tragic contradiction arose. While lust was the major integrative dynamism in life, society struggled against this dynamism and attempted to repress it.

This collision between lust and social repression could be a source of damage to the personality. Lust in the early adolescent promptly collides with a whole variety of other powerful dynamisms in the personality. The most noteworthy collision here is the collision between one's lust and one's need for security, or one's need for social approval. Because society disapproves of the lust dynamism it corrodes one's sense of security, it withdraws approval. For Sullivan, security meant one's feelings of self-esteem and personal worth. As a result, there is the possibility that the young adolescent will suffer a great deal of anxiety because of the thrust and urgency of the newly established sex dynamism. Depending upon prior learning, he can feel dirty, sinful, guilty, or punishable.

Another possibility in regard to the sex dynamism is the confrontation between intimacy and lust. By this Sullivan meant the creating of distinctions between people toward whom lustful desires can apply and people who will be sought for the relief of loneliness. The classical instance in this dichotomy is the old one of the prostitute and the good girl. The prostitute is used to gratify lust, while the good girl is sought out only for friendships or marriage. Satisfying one's lust can be accomplished at considerable expense to one's self-esteem, since the bad girls are unworthy and not really people in the same sense as good girls.

The lust dynamism gives rise to an unfortunate contradiction. In itself, it is one of the most powerful forces for human integration. However, the repressive measure of family and society leads to its distortion. Something that is potentially a healthy phenomena, may become the source of anxiety, guilt and personality warp. Because of the explosive nature of genital awakening in the early adolescent period, this is the period in which most sexual anxieties and maladjustments occur.

6) Late Adolescence

On the basis of the sexual preferences established in early adolescence, the personality advances to that stage in which a recurrent pattern of intersubjective relations harden. Late adolescence is that stage of life in which a personality fixes the manner in which it is to interact with the intersubjective world. With the sexual dynamism in place, the person in late adolescence advances to the standardization of interpersonal modes of behavior. A full personality begins to emerge.

Optimally, the successful negotiations of the stages of infancy, childhood, juvenile period, pre-adolescence and early adolescence would prepare the individual for unhindered growth in his late adolescent period. The achievement of a personality, predictable responses to interpersonal situations, should be an indication that personal growth can proceed in an uncurtailed manner. Unfortunately, this is not the case.

The world of the late adolescent abounds with many opportunities. He has the possibility to expand his horizon by going to school. A career is waiting for him. His social horizons, contacts and general social information is constantly growing. In late adolescence, a person who is not seriously warped in personality and has his sexuality more or less properly functioning and directed, should be in an open-ended growth situation.

Unfortunately a critical opposition can still exist between anxiety, the self-system and growth. Anxiety and the self-system can serve as barriers to continued development.

For example, anxiety can lead to a false personification of the self. By reason of anxiety, the person operates on an inadequate and diminished personification of himself. People come to hold views of themselves which are so far from the truth that their unreasonableness and incongruity are constantly being made evident. A person who is obviously quite intelligent and has accomplished many worthwhile things in the academic world will consider himself as stupid and inadequate. Why can't he see and judge the facts for himself? It is because he is, for some reason, made very anxious by success and achievement. By diminishing one's self-concept, anxiety blocks growth. An individual who is overcome with low self-esteem, is an individual who will not grow.

7) Maturity

In the mature personality, the drive for sex and the need for intimacy are joined. One wants not only the physical gratification of another body, but enjoys the close cooperation and emotional harmony of another person. And in this working together a strong sensitivity to the needs of the other develops. The mature person in the Sullivanian schema will be quite sympathetically understanding of the limitation, interests, possibilities and especially the anxieties of those among whom they move and work. A mature person for Sullivan, is one who has achieved the maximum level of integration with another person. Satisfactory intersubjectivity is the basis of maturity.

Further, the life of the mature, far from becoming closed and limited, is always open and expanding. It is also certain that no person whether mature or terribly underdeveloped can ever escape the possibility of anxiety and fear. The less one is able to tolerate anxiety, the more anxiety becomes an interference with growth and living. But, and this is the important point in Sullivan's schema for development, the greater the degree of maturity, the less will be the interference of anxiety.

For Sullivan, maturity was the condition for the further expanding of the personality. Maturity was not a final stage. It was merely that stage in which the various stages of development culminated, or achieved a harmony: the coordination of the previous stages of growth served as the launching pad for the future enhancement of personality. It was a beginning.

PART FIVE: MENTAL ILLNESS AND SCHIZOPHRENIA

As a therapist and theoretician of mental illness, Sullivan made his greatest contributions in the field of schizophrenia. But schizophrenia is only one species within the larger generic category of mental illness and for that reason we shall begin this part with a discussion of Sullivan's definition of mental illness and then advance to his definition of schizophrenia.

As we mentioned previously, for Sullivan mental health was the ability to maintain adequate and intimate interpersonal relations. Mental sickness, on the other hand, was the failure to establish or preserve satisfactory interpersonal relations. Those processes that hindered satisfactory interpersonal relations he labelled ''dynamisms of difficulty'' and they included selective inattention, the obsessional dynamism, the paranoid dynamism, dissociation, and schizophrenia. Each one of these ''dynamisms of difficulty'' will be discussed below.

Before we begin this analysis, however, it is first necessary to define what Sullivan meant by a ''dynamism of difficulty''. These dynamisms were concerned with the maintenance of security in contrast to the pursuit of satisfaction. The psychic function of ''dynamisms of difficulty'' was protection. The basic drive of the human organism was to find integration and security with its environment, but ''dynamisms of difficulty'' could interfere with this integrative need by means of its preventative function. If a ''dynamism of difficulty'' perceived a threat, which in fact did not exist, it built a barrier between the self and the threat and so blocked any integrative movement between the self and the external. By its learned control over events and stimuli, a ''dynamism of difficulty'' prevented the self from dealing with new stimuli, from learning and growing with new situations and served to imprison the individual into past patterns of behavior. A ''dynamism of difficulty'' was the hold of an earlier period of life over the current period of life. Therefore, the individual was constantly doomed to repeat the past and could not escape it.

The self-system and ''dynamism of difficulty'' shared similar psychiatric tasks: the avoidance of anxiety. Because anxiety is such a powerful danger to the sense of security, any hint of it will trigger the self-system. A mechanism for the safety and preservation of the self, and its sense of security, the self-system will initiate measures to block or contain this incursion of anxiety.

A ''dynamism of difficulty'' performs the same psychic function as the self-system, but differs from the self-system because it is a recurrent pattern of behavior grouped around a particular activity. For example, if we take the phenomena of attention, a ''dynamism of difficulty'' is a repetitive mode of behavior that is centered on the problem of attention.

Selective Inattention

Selective inattention relates to the control of awareness. It is a dynamism that controls the flow of data to our attention. Rather than allowing all data in, selective inattention keeps some data out. The dynamism of selective inattention is a control mechanism that will keep consciousness free of anxiety producing data.

Sullivan made clear that selective inattention had both positive and negative aspects. We all want to avoid anxiety, especially excessive amounts, and selective inattention allows us to do this. But there is also the pathological use of it, because we can lose contact with new data and new situations. If selective inattention filters out too much, if it is activated on too broad a scale, this could dissociate the individual from his environment. Because he is not receiving new data, the individual cannot relate to his environment as it actually appears.

Selective inattention can become a "dynamism of difficulty" because it can impair the process of interaction between the self and its world. One definition of mental illness is that an individual interacts in an inappropriate way to his environment. Selective inattention can become a feature of mental illness if, by preserving the hold of the past over the present, by keeping the individual enslaved to older patterns of behavior, it impairs the ability of the self to interact in a realistic manner to the actual tasks of the present.

The Obsessional Dynamism

The obsessional neurotic plucks out of the tissue of autistic speech of early childhood certain words, phrases, or sentences and uses them as points of preoccupation. In the pursuit of security, the obsessional regresses to certain cognitive operations associated with the stage of autistic speech. The obsessional adult uses what sounds like syntaxic speech to others in an autistic way, that is with very private meanings. The purpose of this repetition, is the immunization from the anxiety occasioned by social threats.

Let us take an example from the early juvenile school years. Little Johnny learns that the right answer to a question will please the teacher. Pleasing the teacher will also disarm him, because he will not have the potential for punishment. Johnny learns that certain actions or words can be very useful in averting punishment and pain. In general, in his "education" through parents and teachers, the child will readily learn what Sullivan calls "the strange power of certain formulas to suspend, nullify, or greatly change what he begins to sense as the simple and natural course of events."[53]

The obsessional dynamism is a form of repetitive ritual. By the recurrent use of words or actions, the individual attempts to control his environment. It bares similarities to the belief in magic.

The Paranoid Dynamism

In discussing paranoia, Sullivan divided this condition into two parts: the paranoid **condition,** and the paranoid **dynamism.**

In the paranoid condition, the individual transfers blame, guilt or responsibility for certain actions and events onto other people. The negative part of the paranoid condition is the presentation of the external world as hostile, or peopled by malevolent enemies. The positive part of the paranoid condition is the protection it renders to individual self-esteem. If the world is responsible for the troubles that a person faces, then that person is exonerated from all guilt and his self-esteem remains intact.

The paranoid condition was ultimately based upon deep feelings of inferiority and inadequacy. One's self-esteem had never been established or was extremely fragile, so it was constantly in a state of being threatened or destroyed by real or imaginary circumstances. For Sullivan, the essence of the paranoid condition was the transference of blame. In order to ward off the agonizing sense of deficiency, the paranoid projects the deficiency onto another person.

The paranoid dynamism is this pattern of behavior of transference. A person with a deficient sense of self believes the following things about himself: "I am inferior, therefore people will dislike me and I cannot be secure with them." Because the individual cannot live with this negative self-assessment, his self-system develops a group of processes that make up the paranoid dynamism. In the paranoid dynamism, one is always the victim of an evil environment.[54] By relocating blame, the paranoid dynamism protects the self from overwhelming feelings of insufficiency. The self-system is the tendency of an organism to maintain its security by protecting itself. A dynamism is self-protection which has assumed a repetitive pattern. A paranoid dynamism is a repetitive pattern of the self-system whose function it is to ward off oceanic feelings of self-deprecation.

The paranoid dynamism totally disrupts the interaction between the self and the environment. The individual cannot learn. Because he cannot learn, because he cannot adjust to new situations, he is a prisoner of his past. He is a slave to an earlier developmental stage that he did not negotiate properly.

Dynamism of Dissociation

By the dissociative dynamism Sullivan referred to the actual dynamic situation by which, for a period of years and perhaps a lifetime, an important system of the personality is effectively detached from a disturbing memory. There is a dissociation between the present concept of self and an anxiety producing past memory. The dynamism of dissociation severs any connection between current consciousness and past trauma. In so doing it preserves the ability of current consciousness to function.

It is because of the severe psychic pain of anxiety and the disabling of life under its influence, that Sullivan assumed that a dynamism of dissociation became a frequent and predominant part of human functioning. It was a dynamism which he said did not disturb the contents of consciousness and it was not an impediment to human activity and the conduct of life. But, in Sullivan's mind, one was more efficient and much nearer happiness if one did not have any important system of personality in dissociation.

The positive aspect of the dynamism of dissociation is that it maintains the self-system and its functioning. The negative aspect of the dynamism of dissociation is that it does not improve anything. It draws people's attention away from unresolved problems and thus leaves them suppressed but intact. It is an effective distraction, but not a cure.

The Schizophrenic Dyanmism

In dealing with the early intellectual influences on Sullivan in Chapter Two of the book I alluded to the work, on schizophrenia by the German psychiatrist Emil Kraepelin on schizophrenia. In that chapter I indicated that William Alanson White and Adolf Meyer revised the somatic conception of Kraepelin concerning the etiology of schizophrenia. Rather than see schizophrenia or "dementia praecox", as Kraepelin referred to it, as solely physiological in origin, both White and Meyer stressed the psychogenic causes of this disease. In this regard, White and Meyer prepared the way for Sullivan, who explained schizophrenia solely in terms of interpersonal relationships.

Kraepelin classified schizophrenia into four categories: the simple, the hebephrenic, the catatonic and paranoid types. The simple type was marked by extreme dissociation between reality and the patients perception of that reality; the hebephrenic form was characterized by a stupor-like state, a condition in which the patient was expressionless and detached; the catatonic version was stamped by great outbursts of rage and the paranoid type was marked by fear of persecution by external forces. Sullivan accepted the Kraepelin classification scheme, but he introduced a new era in the study of schizophrenia by situating its origins in purely interpersonal sources.

According to Sullivan, the onset of schizophrenia coincides with a failure of the self dynamism. The self-dynamism is a protective shield for the personality, and when it ceases to be operative the unitary principle of the "I" collapses. There is nothing to organize the various levels of psychological experience. Repressed aspects of the personality are released. On the other hand, the patient may regress to a much earlier stage of life. The individual can return to infancy and be overcome with the experience of the Good or Bad Mother. The self-system of a thirty-year-old man disintegrates, and he regresses to his infantile period in which he was torn between two personifications of the mother. Two life stages are thus overlapped: chronologically the male is thirty, but emotionally his infantile period has broken through his self-dynamism and his behavior is at the infantile level.

The same process can be defined in a slightly different fashion. The self-dynamism is normally the organizing principle of the personality. In schizophrenia, however, the self-dynamism is repressed. Formerly, the self-dynamism could repress anxiety producing memories of the infantile childhood or juvenile stages, but in schizophrenia the self-system can no longer perform this function. The paralyzing memories of the infantile, childhood and juvenile periods overwhelm consciousness and debilitate the self-dynamism. As a result, the unitary sense of self is shattered, and these diverse stages of the past seize control of his consciousness. The ability of the self to separate itself form the past is destroyed and he is engulfed by it.

The above paragraphs have offered a description of the schizophrenic condition. The preconditions for a schizophrenic break, normally held in check by the self-dynamism, are established during the early stages of personality development and are for the most part associated with the ability to put satisfactory heterosexual relationships in place. In treating young male schizophrenics, Sullivan was convinced that an adolescent's lack of success in making the heterosexual adjustment was of prime importance in causing the schizophrenic break. He believed that the ratio between schizophrenia and pre-adolescent homosexuality was high. Sullivan defined mental health as the ability to put in place satisfactory relations of intimacy, normally of the heterosexual kind. In this process, the pre-adolescent, adolescent and late adolescent stages were critical because the conditions for the healthy relation of intimacy and normal heterosexuality were established during these periods. The origin of schizophrenia dates back to these periods, because if the self cannot successfully negotiate them it is left with a warp that could explode in later life once the self-dynamism disintegrates.

Another typical example of the failure to build satisfactory interpersonal contacts is related to the mother. If an individual entered the pre-adolescent period with a self-personification as a bad-me, or inadequate me in pre-adolescence he was likely to develop an over-dependency on the mother. She became the total source of his self-esteem. For such individuals, neurotic dependency on the mother was very great and an overcoming of such a dependency was extremely difficult. This was even in adult years, for dependent people had the need to create a variety of mother substitutes, either in the form of marriage partners or close friends. When such a development in a boy was extreme, there would be a wholesale incorporation of the mother's values and attitudes. The boy would not be able to progress to a normal interest in girls. Either the mother alone, or some older woman, would be attractive to the boy for what Sullivan calls ''interpersonal intimacies''. Such a boy would not be able to progress smoothly to biologically ordained heterosexuality. As a result, he might be crippled in all of his future interpersonal relations. This course of events will be especially evident in the mid-adolescent stage of personality growth when heterosexual activity and interaction was the norm.

Due to their inability to establish satisfactory interpersonal relationships, these mother-dependent individuals find their social status endangered. They must do something, Sullivan says, to preserve their self-respect and their image with peers. They must either resort to lies about their sexual life or cut themselves off from the general gang and continue a non-heterosexual sociality with other such handicapped (non-developed) individuals. The outcome of such events, because of the increasing pressure of the sexual drive, could well be a homosexual way of life. Or if it does not take this form, they evade the pressure by regressing to an earlier type of interpersonal living which will be a renewed dependence on the parental and related adult environment.[55]

Rationalizing in terms of his own life experiences, Sullivan felt that homosexual encounters were quite frequent occurrences and a recurrent pattern in schizophrenic psychosis. A person arrested in the isophilic or homophilic stage of development in pre-adolescence, offers an example of a regressive retreat from a hopelessly difficult interpersonal situation (heterosexual intimacy) to a time in the past that was actually quite satisfying. Sullivan considered heterosexuality the biologically and socially warranted form of sexuality. While not a warranted or socially sanctioned form of sexuality, homosexuality was frequent, wide-spread and a recurrent symptom of the break-down of heterosexuality. It was a symptom and not an abnormality. Sullivan called it a warp of development.

The existence of a schizophrenic condition entailed the existence of a schizophrenic dynamism. The schizophrenic dynamism demolished the ability of the self to dissociate itself from the anxiety of the past.

In schizophrenia, a conflict developed between the dynamism of schizophrenia and the processes of dissociation. While the processes of dissociation serve to exclude past anxiety from present consciousness, the dynamism of schizophrenia works to include past anxiety. By this inclusion, the schizophrenic dynamism overwhelms the self which is then submerged below the wreckage of the past.[56]

This is the essential relationship of the dissociated dynamism to schizophrenia. The schizophrenic change, for Sullivan, was the inability on the part of the subject "suffering" from one of the three dynamisms, selective inattention, obsessional dynamism, dissociative dynamism, to maintain dissociation. The onset of schizophrenia corresponds to the collapse of any form of dissociation.

PART SIX: METHODS OF TREATMENT

This discussion of Sullivan's methods of treatment will be divided into two parts: A) his theory of the psychiatric interview; B) the ward that Sullivan established at Sheppard-Pratt for the treatment of schizophrenics. Although interrelated Sullivan's philosophy of treatment and his ward at Sheppard-Pratt represent two essentially separate aspects of his treatment methods.

A) The Theory of the Psychiatric Interview

Just as Sullivan's theory of personality growth was based on the notion of interpersonality, so his philosophy of the psychiatric interview also rested upon an interpersonal basis. The psychiatric interview, the fifty minute hour in which the patient and therapist met, was modeled upon a communicative process. For Sullivan, both patient and therapist interacted with each other. The central problem with this conception of the therapy situation was to draw a line between the interaction of the therapist toward the patient, the avoidance of the loss of objectivity on the part of the therapist toward the patient.

Sullivan broke with the Freudian view that in the psychiatric interview the therapist must assume a neutral role. According to Freud, the therapist, while remaining objective, encouraged the transference of the patient. The idea of transference meant that the patient came to look upon the therapist as a significant figure from his own life, transferred onto the therapist attitudes and feelings he harbored towards this significant other person. The therapist remained objective, did not assume the roles which the transferred materials bestowed upon him. But the expression of this transferred material, its articulation, was crucial to the therapy situation because it gave the patient the opportunity to see how primitive attitudes mediated his relations to other people. Once the patient observed his own methods of behavior, once he saw these attitudes actively structure his relationship to another, it would be possible for him to change them.

Sullivan challenged the Freudian notion of presumed objectivity of the therapist. He questioned the fact that it was either possible or desireable for the therapist to detach himself from any subjective involvement with the patient. As opposed to Freud's neutralism and objectivism, Sullivan proposed a theory of participant observation.[57]

According to Sullivan, all life, even the psychiatric interview, was interpersonal in nature. Since it was impossible to delete the subjective from any human situation, the correct posture of the therapist was as a participant observer. This meant that the therapist had to combine two somewhat contradictory roles. The therapist was a participant in that he interacted with the patient: he could not escape the consequences of intersubjectivity. But the therapist must also maintain some distance from the patient, he must represent a viewpoint outside of the intersubjective relationship. Not only must the therapist represent empathy for the patient, but he must also represent reality. Some part of him must remain detached from the interpersonal involvement so that the objective part could reflect the reality of a specific situation back to the patient.

The psychotherapeutic process and specifically the psychiatric interview, in Sullivan's view, was a process_____a never stable movement of interactions taking place between people. In other words, the psychiatric interview was an operational process in which the person observed can be comprehended only in terms of his relationship to others who influence him in his "life space", or field of living, and in terms of the behavior of the observer_____the therapist or interviewer_____who is, of necessity, a part of that field. In Sullivan's thinking there is no situation in which the interviewer is a "neutral" figure in the therapeutic field; he is inevitably a participant and the field of social action is altered by his presence.

In his book, The Psychiatric Interview, Sullivan offered the following definition of the therapy situation:

> *"As I see it, such an interview is a situation of primarily vocal communication in a two-group, more or less voluntarily integrated, on a progressively unfolding expert-client basis for the purpose of elucidating characteristic patterns of living of the subject person, the patient or client, which patterns he experiences as particularly troublesome or especially valuable, and in the revealing of which he expects to derive benefit."[58]*

Sullivan referred to the therapy situation as an "interview" and as an "interrogation." Therapy, for Sullivan, was a situation in which the psychiatrist "interrogated" the patient, within the definition of participant observation, in order to make the patient aware of his repetitive patterns of behavior. The function of the psychiatrist was "interrogation", to ask questions which reveal something about the client to himself. Through dialogue, the psychiatrist leads the patient into the process of self-awareness, and what the patient becomes aware of are his "characteristic patterns of living".[59]

In another passage from the book, *The Psychiatric Interview*, Sullivan expanded on the meaning of the phrase "characteristic patterns of living":

> *To return again to my definition of the psychiatric interviews, I said that it is for the purpose of elucidating characteristic patterns of living. Personality very strikingly demonstrates in every instance, in every situation, the perduring effects of the past; and the effects of a particular past event are not only perhaps fortunate or unfortunate, but also extensively intertwined with the effects of a great many other past events. Thus there is no such thing as learning what ails a person's living, in the sense that you will come to know anything definite, without getting a pretty good idea of who it is that's doing the living, and with whom. In other words, in every case, whether you know it or not, if you are to correctly understand your patients problems, you must understand him in the major characteristics of his dealing with people.''[60]*

A knowledge of a nuclear self-hood was not the final result of the therapy encounter. First of all, Sullivan did not believe in a nuclear self, but rather in an intersubjective plurality of selves. Sullivan wrote about the "myth" of a single self, and rejected Freud's idea of a fixed personality resting upon an intrapsychic Oedipal structure. Sullivan believed in an intersubjective field theory, in which the individual engaged in a multitude of relationships and in which its own self differed in terms of the specific relationship in which it was involved. The end of therapy was not primarily the grasping of a singular "self-hood", but the awareness of behavior. A patient could observe his own behavior, both in the past and in the present. Behavior was something objective, because the patient could "see" it outside himself. Behavior fell into patterns of living, and this was something the patient could change. Self-consciousness was a capacity of thinking, and by observing his own "characteristic patterns of living" the patient could finally come to the realization that it was possible to change them.

Ultimately, the patient would begin to relax his self-system. As we have seen, the self-system was both protection and deterrence. The self-system, by blocking out anxiety provoking situations, arrested the development of an individual at a certain stage. The self-system invoked the activity of a dynamism. Because the self-system was successful in filtering out anxiety situations, the dynamism constantly repeated these blocking patterns. The constant repetitions of these blocking patterns, meant that the patient was doomed to remain a captive of a certain stage of earlier development.

It was Sullivan's expectation that forcing the patient to test reality would dissolve a particularly rigid self-system. The dissolution of the self-system meant that the patient was able to look at reality differently. Without the self-system inherited from the past, he was able to adopt a new mode of relating to reality. Because a new mode existed, he was able to grow.

In general, Sullivan was optimistic about the possibilities of human growth. In this regard, he differed from Freud as well. Of a more pessimistic nature, Freud was convinced of the unwillingness of people to surrender self-destructive behavior patterns. Even though given patterns of behavior could impact individuals acting in such a way as to harm themselves, Freud wondered at the tenacity by which these same people cling to these destructive habits of behavior. Sullivan had a kindlier view of the human potential. According to him, all behavior is the result of two opposing forces. The first force was the self-system or anti-anxiety system which consisted of assumptions, behaviors and processes developed to avoid anxiety. The self-system maintained the hold of the past over the individual. The second force was a drive toward integration and which opened the opportunities for new experience and new growth. It was Sullivan's belief that the forces of integration were strong enough to stimulate future growth.

B) Sullivan's Ward at Sheppard-Pratt

Sullivan initially came to Sheppard-Pratt in 1923, but it was not until 1929 that he established his own ward devoted to the treatment of schizophrenic patients. Sullivan's control over this ward lasted about eighteen months, from 1929 until 1930, when he was let go by Sheppard-Pratt and made his way to New York. As I have shown in Chapter One, Sullivan's creation of this ward was solely due to the backing he received from Ross McClure Chapman.

His success rate with these schizophrenic patients was high, almost 80 per cent. He did not cure them in the sense that schizophrenic symptoms did not return. He was, however, able to alleviate the symptoms of this disease so that his patients were able to leave the hospital and return home. Sullivan's methodology in his ward was mapped out in the 1920's, and there was little attempt to follow-up on these patients. It is not known how many of these patients were able to remain out of the hospital and how many had a recurrence of their disease. Within this definition of success, Sullivan achieved a high rate of patient dismissals from his ward.

Since Sullivan believed that most schizophrenics were either homosexual or had passed through a homosexual episode in pre-adolescence, his ward at Sheppard-Pratt was heavily populated by homosexuals. Although not specifically directed to the treatment of homosexuality, it was devoted to the treatment of schizophrenia, in the onset of which homosexuality was a primary cause.

With Chapman's indulgence, Sullivan ran his ward as a private empire. He had complete control over it, and I will list below the uncontested authority that Sullivan exercised over his ward.

1) Sullivan himself personally selected the entire staff.

2) The entire staff was male.

3) All the patients in the ward were male.

4) Sullivan's ward was independent of the jurisdiction of the nursing unit. In fact, no women were ever allowed on this ward. Sullivan excluded female nurses because he felt that in an all male ward the registered female nurse would be the prototype of the high-status female. When confronted with such a female, the patients would see themselves as a part of an inferior male society and this would contribute to the low self-esteem of the patient and so worsen their illness.

5) Sullivan personally picked all the male attendants and trained them thoroughly to become full-fledged assistants. As such, a high espri de corps developed among them and they came to operate in a truly professional manner and even held their own informal staff conferences.

6) Sullivan believed that a certain type of personality was needed to work with schizophrenics. This is why Sullivan felt that mental health professionals, including doctors, psychiatrists and nurses, were totally inadequate and incapable for the job. He therefore excluded highly trained professionals from his ward.

7) Since Sullivan felt that a certain personality type was required to work well with schizophrenics, he insisted that he pick his staff and then train them. He turned to sub-professionals to interact with his patients because he believed that sub-professionals would most likely have the personality type most suitable to work with schizophrenics.

8) Teamwork of all those involved in the treatment of schizophrenic patients was essential.

9) In essence, Sullivan's idea of therapeutic effectiveness, the treatment milieu for schizophrenics, was a coordinated group consisting of physicians and sub-professional personnel_____nursing, physiotherapist, recreational and occupational_____all selected on the basis of personality make-up suited for dealing with schizophrenics. His concept of a treatment milieu was totalistic: treatment must concern every phase of life inclusive of mental, physical and occupational dimensions.

10) According to eye-witness accounts of former employees, expressions of physical intimacy were allowed between patients and staff.

11) None of the eye-witness accounts attest to any actual genital contact.

12) Some of the eye-witness accounts saw instances when patients would hug, embrace and kiss the attendants.[61]

13) Sullivan believed that homophylic intimacy (perhaps including homosexual activity) leading to heterosexual intimacy was a stage to be lived and worked through, and that such a phase of development, when arrested at the homophylic - homosexual stage, could lead to schizophrenia. Sullivan's theory of therapy was an attempt to remedy this, to show these patients that they were not inhuman for such feelings and activities.

14) Sullivan permitted patients to express physical intimacy with attendants in order to prove to them that they need not feel rejected, odd, embarrassed or humiliated.

From a therapeutic sense, Sullivan's ward was devoted to the re-establishment of pre-adolescent chum relationships. In the life history of the personality, the pre-adolescent stage preferably laid the basis for healthy heterosexual relationships. Failure to create healthy heterosexual contacts opened the door to homosexual exploration. In his ward, Sullivan sought to reproduce chum-relationships to give his patients another opportunity to successfully negotiate this stage a second time. By the re-creation of the chum experience Sullivan hoped to supply his patients with enough support to enable them to build sound heterosexual love, to overcome the homosexual arrestation and to move beyond schizophrenia.

This is what Sullivan meant by milieu, the recapturing of the essential characteristics of the chum period. In order to recapture the basic milieu of the chum, Sullivan permitted touching and kissing between staff and patients. (Anyone interested in more detailed accounts of the structure and operation of Sullivan's ward at Sheppard-Pratt is advised to consult the unpublished doctoral dissertation of Kenneth L. Chatelaine. This dissertation contains extensive quotes form eye-witnesses who attest to the procedures in the ward. It has ample documentation, including recorded analytic sessions between Sullivan and some of his patients. It is a rich reservoir of Sullivaniana.)

On June 18, 1930, Sheppard-Pratt dismissed Sullivan. Chapman could not protect him any longer. The official reason given for dismissal was insufficient funds to continue the work of the ward. In all probability, he was dismissed because the hospital administration suspected the existence of homosexual practices.

CHAPTER FOUR

SULLIVAN'S PLACE IN AMERICAN PSYCHIATRY

The philosophic basis of Sullivan's psychiatry was grounded in the disciplines of social psychology and Einsteinian physics. From the discipline of social psychology, Sullivan learned the theory of interpersonality, the idea that man and society were inseparable and engaged in a continuous process of reciprocal influence. From Einsteinian physics, Sullivan learned to look upon the intersubjective world between man and man in terms of a field theory. A field, a society, was composed of an infinite number of relationships, and an individual who was situated in a field must be seen as a composite of intersecting relationships. Sullivan offered an Einsteinian view of the self, a theory of the self as relativistic, as a vector of a multitude of personal and societal relationships. Sullivan's acquaintance with the theory of relativity was probably an outgrowth of his early interest in physics. When Sullivan first entered Cornell University he wished to study physics, and obviously this interest remained with him for the rest of his life.

Sullivan stood in the forefront of the movement in the 20th Century that wished to bring about a juncture between psychiatry and the other social sciences. Sullivan was groping toward a unified theory of the social sciences. Assuming that psychiatry was primary, Sullivan believed that the collaboration of the other social sciences and psychiatry would create a totalistic approach to the study of man. Accepting the need for interdisciplinary research and work, Sullivan argued that only a unified theory of the functioning of man and society was capable of explaining the behavior of man or society.

Sullivan's initial movement toward a unified theory of the social sciences occurred in the 1920's under the impress of the Chicago University School of Sociology, Cooley and Mead for the most part. It was only when Sullivan became aware of the importance that social psychology had for psychology that he became an advocate of the interdisciplinary fusion of psychiatry and the social sciences. In order to be understood properly, Sullivan's contributions in this area must be compared to the work, for example, of Harold Lasswell. Also beginning in the 1920's, Lasswell worked for the juncture of psychology and political science. Lasswell initiated the psychoanalytic interpretation of political behavior. This was a broad movement, and Sullivan was a pioneer in this field.

Freud had initiated the psychoanalytic interpretation of culture. Although Sullivan, like Freud, wished to understand the psychological basis of culture, he did not want to understand psychoanalytically. He did not want to apply Freudian categories to the analysis of society. The categories that Sullivan preferred to apply were drawn from social psychology. Sullivan did not believe in an oedipal interpretation of religion (the thesis of Freud's <u>Totem and Taboo</u>) but he did believe that society was the primary force molding the human personality and that it was possible to understand individual psychology in terms of the social categories which shaped it.

The line of development in which Sullivan stood stretched from Harold Lasswell to Edward Sapir to Karen Horney and Erich Fromm. Karen Horney also wrote extensively on anxiety, and Erich Fromm tried to point out the social determination of human personality. In his book, *Escape from Freedom,* Fromm attempted to show how cultural attitudes in Germany prepared the way for Fascism. Wilhelm Reich made the same effort in his study *The Mass Psychology of Fascism.* Both Fromm and Reich believed that the success of Hitler in Germany rested upon the social psychology of the German people, their socially induced respect for authority and their passive attitude toward father-figures. Sullivan was one of the leaders of this trans-Atlantic movement that gathered steam in the 1920's and 1930's in Europe and America. Sullivan must be seen as one of the pioneers in this movement to apply psychological insights, predicated on social psychological definitions, to the study of human history and social development.

Another philosophical presupposition of Sullivanian psychology was the idea of historicity or evolution. A paramount intellectual motif in the 20th Century was the idea of process. Sullivan took this idea of historicity and used it as an analytic tool to understand the human personality and the self. Two major philosophers of the 20th Century focused on the notions of time and change. These ideas formed the core of Martin Heideggers <u>Being and Time</u> and Jean-Paul Sartre's <u>Being and Nothingness</u>. Sullivan was not a philosopher, but the fact that he also recognized the importance of the idea of historicity shows that he was responding to the deepest intellectual currents of the 20th Century.

The application of the idea of historicity to the problem of personality led to Sullivan's theory of the developmental stages of human growth. Just as history and society were governed by process, so the personality in itself was in a constant process of becoming.

Sullivan's application of the idea of process to personality helped produce a major change in the understanding or personality. Sullivan's epigenetic hypothesis annulled the notion of a fixed and permanent personality structure. Instead of a nuclear personality, Sullivan presented an interpretation of personality as evolutionary.

Sullivan's breakthrough in the theory of personality forced a revision of previous Freudian notions. Whereas Freud saw the personality as being formed by the juvenile stage, Sullivan looked upon the pre-adolescent and adolescent stages as primary. Whereas Freud saw personality as being formed as a result of the oedipal conflict, Sullivan saw personality as essentially molded in the confusions regarding homosexual or heterosexual preference during the pre-adolescent and adolescent periods. Sullivan's evolutionary theory of the personality anticipated the work of Erik Erikson.

Sullivan's theory of personality helped fundamentally alter modern conceptions of personality. It was no longer understood in the Freudian sense, as a drama in which adults were doomed and sentenced to repeat the oedipal conflicts of their early life. Sullivan presented a view of personality associated with the idea of capacity, the belief that life was continuous growth and unfolding.

When Sullivan applied the idea of historicity to the self, he did away with the category of a nuclear self. The body helped create the illusion of a single self. The body, because it was identifiable (it had red hair and blue eyes) created the impression that it was only inhabited by one self. The notion of historicity when it was joined to the question of self, showed that many selves, stemming from the different developmental stages, inhabited a single body.

The dissolution of the nuclear self received confirmation from the Einsteinian idea of a field, which Sullivan re-interpreted to mean social field. The fusion of the concept of historicity and social field, demolished the idea of a nuclear self. Not only was the self a product of time, but it was also a product of place. Not only was the self subject to change, but it also changed in terms of the relationships in which it was entrapped.

Einstein used the idea of field in relation to physics, but Sullivan related it to society. Sullivan's notion of self paralleled Einstein's notion of relativity. According to Einstein, the velocity of an object was determined by the relationship in which that object stood to other objects. The Einsteinian world was a world of mirrors. What a person saw of himself depended on which mirror he was facing. Similarly, Sullivan's theory of the self was a form of identity relativity. The personification a person had of himself depended upon the person or social context to which an individual related. Just as there were an infinite number of possible relationships in a society, so there were a multiple of selves that emerged out of this context. Sullivan's theory of the self can be referred to as identity contextuation. The image of the self was reflection of the context in which it was embedded.

The theory of anxiety also played a significant role in the Sullivanian system. Sullivan did not invent this idea, for we have seen that he was influenced by Freud and Kempf on this issue. But within Sullivanian psychiatry it slipped forth as a major philosophical presupposition.

The emphasis that Sullivan placed on anxiety undoubtedly was conditioned by historical circumstances Sullivan experienced during the most chaotic times of the 20th Century. Born in 1892, Sullivan was 31 when Mussolini came to power. He was 41 when Hitler came to the pinnacle of the German state. The Second World War began in 1939, and Sullivan was 47. These major revolutions of the 20th Century uprooted old certainties and new certainties had not yet been formed. The poet W. H. Auden referred to this historical epoch as an ''age of anxiety''. Not only were there personal and scientific reasons for Sullivan's exploration into the phenomena of anxiety, but the cacophonous world of the 20th Century was itself anxiety producing. Sullivanian psychiatry was a child of its time. It reflected a world order to total collapse.

Even though Sullivan lived during revolutionary times when the prevailing cultural syndrome was despair, he never lost hope. In this regard, he was the child of the Enlightenment. His faith in the human potential was shown in his downplay of the Freudian notions of the unconscious and free association. A product of the cultural pessimism of the 19th and 20th Centuries, Freud focused on the role of the unconscious in the determination of human life. Through the use of free association, Freud believed that it was possible to make contact with the unconscious and release hidden early childhood oedipal traumas. The unconscious, for Freud was a vast storehouse of repressed and anxiety provoking memories, which had a great impact in the causation of human behavior. Freud's hard realism was shown by the fact that he assigned such great importance to a realm of the human mind which was so inaccessible to conscious investigation and control.

The unconscious and free association played a less significant role in Sullivanian psychiatry. Therapy, for Sullivan, was not directed at recovering unconscious motivations. In Sullivanian psychiatry therapy was more presentest. Its aim was to have the patient face reality and attempt to alter behavior. Sullivan questioned free association, but embraced interrogation. To free associate meant to pursue the labyrinth of interwoven words and memories back to the past, while to interrogate was to thrust reality at the patient in the hope that he could alter behavior. The therapeutic hour was not designed for self-revelation, but for self-modification. Sullivan was not as concerned with the unconscious, as with the will to get well.

The advances that Sullivan made in the treatment of schizophrenia, also displays his Enlightenment belief in human improvement. Even though Sullivan's ward at Sheppard-Pratt raises some medical and ethical questions, he was still one of the first to apply psychoanalysis to the treatment of schizophrenia. Kraepelin thought that schizophrenia was somatic in origin and therefore inaccessible to therapeutic treatment. Freud thought that psychoanalysis was inapplicable to the treatment of schizophrenia. Leaving aside the question of Sullivan's method of treatment, he was still one of the first to explore the use of psychoanalysis of a tool of therapy. He brought hope to the ill. If we put aside the question of the effectiveness of Sullivan's treatment on a long term basis, not only was Sullivan one of the first to introduce psychoanalysis in the treatment of schizophrenia, but he also showed that it was an efficacious instrument of treatment.

This summary of the major contributions of Sullivan, shows that he significantly helped advance American psychiatry. On the philosophical level, Sullivan brought American psychiatry into contact with some of the dominant intellectual trends of the 20th Century. Sullivan made American psychiatry think the concepts of historicity, evolution, interpersonality, field theory and anxiety. When American psychiatry made contact with these 20th Century philosophical ideas, it became a better medical movement. Sullivan insured that some of the major philosophical ideas of the 20th Century entered into the lexicon of American psychiatry. When Sullivan did this he guaranteed that American psychiatry would be a more powerful therapeutic instrument. It is only by absorbing and distilling the new ideas of an age that a single discipline like psychiatry can grow. Sullivan's key role was as a transmitter of ideas: by taking current philosophical ideas into the vocabulary and practice of psychiatry, he made certain that American psychiatry aligned itself with the most recent advances in the sciences and philosophy. But he paid a price. The tradationalists would see to it. His last words to his foster son, James Inesco Sullivan, on January 2, 1949 just before leaving for Amsterdam and The International Conference on World Peace are his final will and testament:

I probably will not return. But remember this and do not forget it. I shall be controversial. There was no way to avoid it.

GOOD ME, BAD ME, NOT ME

REFERENCES

[1] Sullivan, Harry Stack, <u>Personal Psychopathology</u> (New York, 1965), p. 180.
[2] Perry, Helen Swick, <u>Psychiatrist of America</u> (Cambridge, 1982), p. 45.
[3] Chapman, A. H., <u>Harry Stack Sullivan</u> (New York, 1976), p.20
[4] Perry, p. 58.
[5] Chatelaine, Kenneth Leo, <u>Harry Stack Sullivan: The Formative Years</u> (Unpublished Ph.D. Dissertation, University of Maryland, 1978).
[6] Perry, pp. 76-81.
[7] Chapman, 23.
[8] <u>Ibid.</u>
[9] Sullivan, <u>Personal Psychopathology</u>, pp. 198-199.
[10] In addition, corroborating evidence for this thesis was found by Kenneth L. Chatelaine. In his unpublished dissertation, Chatelaine provides evidence that Sullivan was hospitalized at Binghampton State Mental Hospital during these years. For further documentation, readers are directed to Chatelaine's doctoral dissertation.
[11] <u>Ibid</u>, p. 35.
[12] Chatelaine, Kenneth Leo, <u>Harry Stack Sullivan: The Formative Years</u>.
[13] Perry, p. 413.
[14] Collins, Randal, and Makowsky, Michael, <u>The Discovery of Society</u> (New York, 1989), p. 183.
[15] <u>Ibid</u>, p. 184.
[16] Crowley, R, "Harry Stack Sullivan: His Contribution to Current Psychiatric Thought and Praxis", in <u>Major Contributions to Modern Psychotherapy</u> (New Jersey, 1971), p. 145.
[17] Chatelaine, <u>Harry Stack Sullivan: The Formative Years</u> (1892-1930), pp. 163-164.
[18] <u>Ibid</u>, p. 318.
[19] <u>Ibid</u>, p. 264.
[20] <u>Ibid</u>, p. 270.
[21] <u>Ibid</u>, p. 320.
[22] <u>Ibid</u>, p. 316-364.
[23] Sullivan, "The Interpersonal Theory of Psychiatry", in <u>The Collected Works of Harry Stack Sullivan</u> (New York, 1953), Vol I, p. 34.
[24] <u>Ibid</u>, p. 36.
[25] <u>Ibid</u>, p. 103.
[26] <u>Ibid</u>, pp. 110-111.
[27] <u>Ibid</u>, p. 80.
[28] Chatelaine, pp. 58-77.
[29] Sullivan, "The Interpersonal Theory of Psychiatry", p. 160.
[30] <u>Ibid</u>, pp. 161-163.
[31] <u>Ibid</u>, pp. 92-98.

[32] Ibid, p. 166.

[33] Sullivan, ''The Illusion of Personal Individuality'', <u>Psychiatry</u> (Vol 13, 1950), pp. 317-332.

[34] Ibid, p. 95.

[35] Sullivan, <u>The Psychiatric Interview</u>, (New York, 1954), p. 102.

[36] Sullivan, ''The Interpresonal Theory of Psychiatry'', p. 9.

[37] Ibid., p. 43.

[38] Ibid, p.43.

[39] Ibid, pp. 379-380.

[40] Ibid, p. 115.

[41] Ibid, p. 352.

[42] Ibid, p. 11.

[43] Ibid, p. 11-12.

[44] Ibid.

[45] Sullivan, ''The Interpersonal Theory of Psychiatry'', Vol I, p. 300.

[46] Ibid, p. 33.

[47] Ibid.

[48] Ibid, p. 34.

[49] Chatelaine, p. 335.

[50] Sullivan, ''Conceptions of Modern Psychiatry'', Vol I, p. 44.

[51] Chatelaine, p. 108.

[52] Ibid.

[53] Ibid, p. 109.

[54] Sullivan, <u>Clinical Studies in Psychiatry</u>, Vol II, p. 28.

[55] Chatelaine, p. 346.

[56] Ibid, pp. 324-328.

[57] Ibid, p. 359.

[58] Sullivan, <u>The Psychiatric Interview</u>, Vol I, p.4.

[59] Ibid, p. 13.

[60] Ibid.

[61] Chatelaine, p. 405.

INDEX

GOOD ME, BAD ME, NOT ME

GOOD ME, BAD ME, NOT ME

GOOD ME, BAD ME, NOT ME

GOOD ME, BAD ME, NOT ME

GOOD ME, BAD ME, NOT ME

GOOD ME, BAD ME, NOT ME